Horses for Courses:
The Definitive Guidebook for the Prospective College Equestrian

RANDI C. HEATHMAN

ISBN: 1500473545
ISBN-13: 978-1500473549

For my parents – my first and finest educators

CONTENTS

PREFACE

Each year, passionate young equestrians like you spend untold hours in the saddle. You're enthusiastic. You're enthralled by the sport and passionate about horses. This focused joy is what drives you to want to perfect your skills so that you can become better and better. As time goes on, your goals increase with your training and experience:

"I want to jump higher."

"I want to do a canter pirouette for a nine."

"I want to ride at Rolex."

For young equestrians like you, each upcoming competition is viewed in the same vein as the Olympics and, whether it's the North American Junior and Young Rider Championship or a schooling show at your home barn, your commitment to excellence is unwavering.

Does this sound familiar? Are you this rider? Or is this rider perhaps your daughter, son, niece, nephew, or grandchild?

If you answered "yes" to any of those questions, thank you for picking up this book. If you *are* one of those young and talented riders I just described, you know the feeling of setting the bar very high for yourself and for your horse. You understand that it doesn't matter if your goal for the year is to win at the local county fair, an open show through 4-H, or if you hope to help your team make it to IEA Nationals for the first time. You also understand that it doesn't matter if the goal goes beyond that – that you hope to compete internationally at the NAJYRC or even the Olympic Games. **No matter how large or small the goals are, the commitment that you have to being the best possible rider you can is all-encompassing; you accept nothing but the best from yourself every day.**

With such focus, there can be no doubt that your commitment to the sport is total. Chances are you spend every available moment of your afterschool hours and weekends at the barn. You talk nonstop about horses and horse-related topics with your friends and, outside of the time spent on homework and with family, yours is a full schedule that is packed with horses, riding, and more horses. Celebrities to you aren't the Kardashians, Ryan Gosling, or Lorde – they're people like Reed Kessler, Steffen Peters, and Boyd Martin.

What's more, you wouldn't have it any other way.

It's inspiring for the adults around you and your fellow young equestrians to watch you take such pride in your sport and for them to see what fantastic luck you have to get to participate in a sport that isn't accessible to everyone – a sport that quite honestly doesn't even *appeal* to everyone. Riding is a sport that isn't as "simple" as running the fastest or kicking a ball into a goal in order to score points.

(As an instructor friend of mine teases his students, "Riding is supposed to be hard; if it wasn't, they'd call it bowling.")

Unquestionably, equestrian sports are worlds different from other athletic activities that you might find on your school's list of varsity sports. Riding is also made more challenging by the fact that your most important teammate doesn't even communicate verbally. To become a skilled horseman therefore requires a unique set of abilities, sensibilities, and coordination on the part of the person in the saddle - so it's not surprising to see that the success you find as a rider can give you a sense of confidence and responsibility that is greater than that of athletes who play more traditional sports.

(After all, how many basketball players do you know whose teammates are entirely dependent on them for every single part of their living situation - from practice and competition to meals, medical needs, housing needs, clothing needs, and everything in between on each and every day of the year?)

Sadly though, as you and your friends enter high school and the time to transition to college approaches, a change often occurs. It may not have happened to you yet, but you might have an indication that it's on the horizon. I refer to that inevitable moment when the out-of-the-box nature of equestrian competition - previously an important point of pride that differentiated you from your classmates – becomes more problematic than special. Around you, the friends who play soccer and lacrosse begin to discuss scholarship opportunities and compare the advantages and disadvantages of playing in NCAA Divisions I, II, and III while they dream out loud about what their college playing careers will be like. Coaches and college counselors seem to already know how to help them put together recruitment videos and athletic resumes to send to college coaches for review. Everything looks to be falling into place with the greatest of ease.

Meanwhile for you, riding remains a sport that won't fit into the same box as that of a traditional sport - even as much as you and your guidance counselor would like to fold it until it fits neatly within the parameters.

Do you wonder if you are the only one who doesn't understand how to make the leap to becoming a college equestrian? You've read about riders who are recruited to join college teams and you've even heard about students who earn riding scholarships to help offset the costs of going to school, but is that a realistic possibility for you to look into? And if so, where should you even begin?

Perhaps author Lewis Carroll said it best in *Alice in Wonderland*:

"Begin at the beginning," the King said, very gravely, "and go on till you come to the end: then stop."'

But where is the beginning?

From where you sit, there appears to be no clear pipeline for you to follow into a college equestrian career the way there is for the boys who play football or your best friend who plays point guard on the basketball team. It's doubtful that your guidance counselor or any of your teachers can lend assistance beyond pointing you in the approximate direction of some web sites that feature "colleges with horses." Equestrian sports are incredibly diverse – as is the college landscape itself – and there are a lot of paths you can take to reach your goals. Some of the paths seem well-trod and fairly straightforward, but others are overgrown and look as though you'll need to force your way through if you want to get to the other side. By now, you might even be frustrated enough to think that the very differences that have always made riding so special for you look like nothing but a potential problem for your college years if you want to move to the next level - or even if you simply just want to define what that "next level" might be in the first place.

Meanwhile, if you're a parent and are reading this book in search of guidance so that you can better support your child, you may have begun to wonder if there's any way that all of the lessons and shows that you've dutifully paid for since your young rider was in kindergarten or since she came home excited from summer camp in the fifth grade can now help pay a return on your investment. Can riding earn your son or daughter an athletic scholarship to help cushion your financial burden when the first tuition bill arrives? Or even if there's no money in it, is riding a so-called "hook" that can help give your student an edge when it comes to getting accepted to a highly selective school in the middle of an increasingly challenging college admissions race?

Students and parents alike – take heart. The college process tends to overwhelm everyone the first time they go through it and it doesn't matter if the student is an equestrian, a scientist, a baseball player, or first oboe in the school orchestra. *Everyone* is uncertain, confused, and downright scared when they're first starting out. (Students, remember your first horse show? It's that same feeling all over again – the fear of wanting to show yourself at your very best while not fully comprehending what's about to be asked of you.)

Some families face the situation head on and throw everything they possibly can into the pot in an effort to come out with something recognizable and useful at the end. I've seen it happen on numerous occasions: young riders and their parents see the beacon of college beckoning on the horizon and immediately seek to create an equation where *riding talent* + *the right college and coach* = *a full ride scholarship* (no pun intended) to a dream school.

And in order to make this situation a reality, the family does everything within their power to make sure that the student does all of "the right things" in order to be actively recruited by "the best" coach and "the best" college – even though the definition of "best" varies drastically by family. Horses are purchased or sold; trainers are hired or fired; horse show calendars are arranged, rearranged, and then rearranged some more - and all because families cobble together as many credible sources on the topic of riding in college that they're able to find and forge their way onto that path without any idea of what they will find at the end of it.

What's most frustrating is that the unfortunate result of this aimless scramble is often a college search that can't help but be *re*active as opposed to proactive. "The right" schools to apply to tend to be chosen after hasty Internet searches for "college equestrian team" or "equine college;" campus visits are scheduled only after the student receives acceptance letters in the spring of senior year; and the final decision has to be made in a hurry before the students or parents have a sense that they've thoroughly investigated all of their options. In fact, most lack the time and appropriate knowledge to understand the mechanics of riding in college altogether, so the decision on where the student will enroll winds up based on limited information of all of the possible opportunities. Many families don't know what they've overlooked but also don't have the luxury of enough time to figure out what's missing because enrollment deposits must be sent by a firm deadline if the student will enroll *anywhere* in the fall.

But what if there was a way to be *pro*active in your search for a college as a student equestrian right from Day One? What if you could begin to investigate potential schools with a guide in your hand that would outline how exactly what steps you can take to make your search a successful one? Wouldn't that be better than forging a trail on your own?

This book is that guide and its goal is simple:

It aims to walk you through the college search process from beginning to end as both a prospective *student* and as a prospective college equestrian. From the first moment that you consider the idea of going to college to the day you send your enrollment deposit and begin to plan the decoration scheme for your dorm room, this book will lay a path before you that can help get you to where you want to be with the least amount of challenges, confusion, and roadblocks along the way.

Please bear in mind that this book is not the be all and end all of college guides. It's not an outline of advanced strategies that can help you gain admission to the most selective Ivy League schools in the country and it's certainly not a step-by-step explanation of "This is How You Get Recruited to Ride in College." What's more, within these pages you won't find insider tricks to make equestrian coaches like you or incent them to give you scholarship money.

When you finish the final chapter, you won't find a listing of all of the colleges and universities in the United States and Canada that have equestrian teams and programs because this most certainly isn't a Zagat guide to "the best" equestrian programs to be found on the market today. (Other books have already been written on all of the previously-mentioned topics and there are a host of wonderful web resources that can provide you with much of that information as well.)

Instead, the book in your hand is an examination of the current college landscape for equestrians and an outline that will help you assess your own talents and goals coming out of high school to help you determine what you want your college riding career to look like – as well as your life during and *after* college. Along the way, you will be asked to think about what types of academic and non-riding extracurricular activities you wish to experience as a college student, what's most important to you when it comes to your education, and what you want the career outcome to be when you've finished your degree. In some ways, this book is really more of a beginner's instruction manual on the college search – how you can take ownership of it for yourself and how you can move forward in your riding career at the same time or instead use your college years to experience new types of riding.

Within these pages are descriptions of the major college equestrian organizations that currently operate in the United States, some information concerning scholarship awarding practices for riders (and non-riders too), outlines of the expectations of most coaches and their general recruiting timelines, things to think about if you plan to take your own horse along with you or leave it at home, as well as other riding-related topics. But beyond the equestrian side of the equation, I'll also share strategies and recommendations for your general college search, for completing your essay and application during senior year, and for evaluating your final college choices. I'll begin with how to make a list of potential schools and move through the considerations you'll need to consider when it comes to balancing the academic, equestrian, and social sides of your busy life. I also spoke with current and former college equestrians before I sat down to write this book so that they could pass on stories and things they wish they had known when they became college equestrians. There is much you can learn from their advice as well.

Even though this book is designed as a map to take you on a

guided journey from your current location (high school) to a new destination (college), you can read it in any order that you prefer. If you like, you can follow the chapters numerically through the college search and application process and use the information to guide you every step of the way. Or if you would rather, simply turn directly to the chapters that most relate to you and skip over the ones that don't. But no matter how you choose to read through these pages, it is my hope that by the time you set the book down, you'll feel as though you better understand the school options that are available to you, your college riding options, and you'll know how to find the ones that will best fit you.

Even with this guide in your hand, however, you'll still need some outside help and support along the way. A trusted teacher, the college counselor at your high school, or an independent educational consultant should spend time helping you pore over your school options, make sure that you're keeping in line with all important deadlines, and assist you in putting your very best self on display in your applications before they're sent off. Along the way, he or she can also help answer your questions as they arise and use their years of experience and expertise to make the process as smooth as possible for you.

And if you don't have a teacher or educational professional who is able to assist you, seek help from your trainer, a mentor, or even a pastor/minister – anyone who knows you well and wants to help you succeed will be a good resource for you to reach out to when you need encouragement.

Riding is one of those wonderful sports that can last for a lifetime if you want it to. As you turn the pages of this book, remember that, while college is a hugely transformational experience in your young life, it's also just a stopping point that helps you determine who you are and what direction you would like to take as you step into adulthood. Every journey must begin somewhere and your journey from high school equestrian to college equestrian begins with the first chapter of this book.

IS COLLEGE THE RIGHT CHOICE FOR ME?

"If you were a good student in high school (like most equestrian people are), it's not impossible or excessively hard to balance riding and going to school and working. You have to choose your priorities and how you spend your time but you are able to work ride and be successful in school!"
Ann, IHSA hunt seat and IDA dressage equestrian

Admittedly, it seems strange to begin a book about the search for the right college (and college equestrian situation) with the question, "Is college the right choice for me?" If you truly want to begin your college quest at square one, however, you must first understand what your purpose for going to college will be in the first place. It's also important for you to have an idea about how a college degree will play a role in helping you to achieve your future goals. After all, if you were a horse trainer, you wouldn't expect a green horse that's never jumped a fence in its life to suddenly pop over a four foot oxer on command, would you? Instead, you'd start with the fundamentals; you'd lay out ground poles before working up to crossrails, then add real fences and so on. Only *after* you'd solidified these basic skills would you take the young horse out and point him at a full course of fences because only then would you know without a doubt that he was mentally and physically prepared to face the challenge.

Your college search should begin the same way – with a series of ground poles and crossrails that teach you to think about college in general terms before you work your way up to the more specific items that will be a part of your individual search for the right school. As with the horse that's learning to jump, your initial understanding of what going to college means for your career prospects down the road will lay the foundation for everything that will follow. In particular, as the costs of attending college continue to rise each year, you don't want to put yourself in a position where you invest a substantial amount of tuition dollars into something that you're not even sure that you need or want in the first place. Instead, you must turn yourself into an educated consumer – one who knows exactly what the pros and cons of attending college will be for you and where you want your eventual outcome to take you.

It isn't crucial right at this moment that you know exactly what you want to be when you grow up. (Many adults will tell you that they *are* grownups and still don't know – but that's a story for another book.) You're still very young and there are a host of academic subjects and career possibilities that you haven't even been exposed to yet - though there's a good chance that you've given at least a little thought to your future as the end of high school approaches. Maybe a teacher or guidance counselor has helped along the way by administering a career diagnostic tool to your class or maybe you've had conversations with your parents or with friends about your interests.

Regardless of the state of your current career ambitions, take a moment right now to consider what your life after high school will look like: What do you see yourself doing in five years? How about in ten years? Do you already possess a set of skills that you'd like to perfect in a certain field or area? Is there a subject in school that your teachers moved past very quickly but that you'd like to take the time to study in-depth? Do you know someone with an interesting job that you think you might like to try one day?

If you're still completely undecided at this point or are interested in so many different things that you don't know how you're going to narrow your choices down just yet, that's okay too. Though many arguments have been published recently in favor of strict career preparation for students as opposed to more liberal and varied study at the collegiate level, it really isn't necessary to know exactly what career path you want to pursue before you go to college. There are so many potential college majors available to you – the majority of which aren't taught at the high school level – that you'll have far more opportunities to explore the ones that interest you once you're an enrolled college student. (In fact, one of the purposes for going to college in the first place is to discover what these different fields are all about and if any of them are a fit for you.)

Perhaps an easier question for you to answer right now is simply what you would like your own adulthood to look like; do you see yourself married with kids and career that you enjoy? Do you want to travel? Where would you like to live – in the country on a horse farm or somewhere in the city? Is your riding career going to expand after college or is it something that might be scaled back for a bit?

Once you've examined the whole picture as from your current perspective, take a moment to think about what steps you'll need to take to make that lifestyle into a reality: What skills will you need to acquire? What type of financial decisions will you be faced with? What day-to-day responsibilities will be included with the dream you have for yourself? And what part (or parts) of your path might require you to have a college degree?

If you're already overwhelmed at such thinking and all of the planning that goes with it, you're not alone. The thought of graduating high school – whether you're headed for college or not – is a huge milestone in every young person's life and it marks your first real transition into adulthood in a lot of ways. It's scary and can seem daunting at first, but many students have trod the path that lies before you and many will follow after you as well. It will take careful planning on your part to ensure you understand exactly why you're making the decisions that you must – just as the identification of your ultimate goal allows you to keep a target in sight as you move forward. Likewise, it's this type of methodical progression that helps to ease the sting of transition.

(Remember the ground poles and crossrails? This is what they look like for high school students.)

For the majority of high school students, the transition to complete adulthood is postponed by a trip to college for a few years. In fact, in 2013, 21.8 million students were expected to attend colleges and universities in the United States and there's a good chance that you and your parents have expected you to join that number all along. Perhaps as early as your elementary school days, your mom and dad talked about your future in terms of, "When you're in college…" or gave descriptions of the types of classes you might take or the various activities that you can participate in as a college student. Maybe during holiday gatherings family members have shared their own stories of college life or have taken you to visit their alma mater for Homecoming or a class reunion event. You might have older brothers, sisters, cousins, or friends who have already enrolled in college and have shared their experiences and stories with you. (Maybe they've even invited you to campus for a visit during a little siblings event or a family weekend.) No matter where you look, college students and college graduates are all around you, so it's unlikely that this book is your first encounter with the concept.

To simply *assume*, however, that you will blindly sign yourself up for college without understanding why you want to go there in the first place is an idea that is the educational equivalent of deciding that you'll ride the four-star cross-country course at Rolex without benefit of walking the course first. "Oh, I'll just wing it" is a sure way to injure yourself when it comes to cross-country jumping and just as sure a way to mangle your future prospects as you begin the college search.

So, *is* college the right choice for you?

The worst thing you can do for your future is enroll in a college simply because "everyone else is going so I might as well join in." (The second worst thing is to enroll in a college just because it has a riding program so, "At least I'll get to ride while I'm there.")

College is something that you enter with a purpose – even if that purpose is as simple as discovering what subjects you're passionate about. Just as with your daily work with the horses in your life, the journey through higher education can often teach you as much (if not more) than the destination itself – but likewise as in riding, you need to begin with a purpose in order to succeed. When you get on your horse at the beginning of a training session, you have purpose – you're setting out to become a better rider and make your horse more responsive to your cues. Perhaps you have a goal for the day – a better leg yield, a smoother lope depart from the walk - but your horse might dictate that a different area needs your focus on that particular day so the goal must change. Your purpose during that ride is the same and your journey is still moving forward, but for now the destination is different than the one you planned. Finding your chosen career path – as well as selecting the right college to attend – are processes that are very much the same.

If you're the type of student who already knows that you want to go to college because you have a specific goal in mind but you don't still know where to begin your search, you might find it helpful to work backward from your desired outcome to better illuminate the path you should take to get there. If you want to become a physical therapist, for example, you can begin your research by learning that physical therapists have to be board certified and licensed in order to practice - which they gain after going through an accredited graduate program in physical therapy. Before you can enroll in a graduate program in physical therapy, however, you'll need an undergraduate degree in kinesiology or another similar health or science-related field to gain admission; as such, you'll want to look for a college or university with very strong health or exercise science programs and you'll want the college itself (location, price, acceptance rate) to match up with the other factors that have priority in your college search (such as having a riding team, being within three hours of your current home, and having less than two thousand students in the undergraduate population). You'll also want to make sure that your high school science grades (as well as all of your other coursework) are as good as they can be so that your application for the college will be accepted. It's a linear process that falls easily into place once you identify each step that needs to occur along the way.

If you're not that focused yet on one specific career idea and remain completely undecided as to what program of study interests you, yours is a journey that you won't travel alone. In 2012, eighty percent of the freshman students at Pennsylvania State University revealed that they were undecided as to what they wanted to study. What's more, included in the population surveyed were students who had already declared a major! In addition, the National Center for Education Statistics reports that eighty percent of all college students will change their major at least once before they finish college - and that the average college student will change majors *three* times between freshman year and graduation. (Remember, a college education introduces students to subject areas and potential career fields they haven't previously heard of so it's no wonder that so many wind up pursuing majors they never planned on as high school seniors!)

What's the conclusion to be drawn from the above data? If you're undecided about your path of study as a college freshman, not only will you be in good company with many of your classmates, but you will also be free to explore classes that sound interesting to you in an effort to determine what you will eventually turn your full focus to. It's a wonderful opportunity and might help you discover a new interest or talent that you never knew you had. As long as you know that your purpose for being a college student hasn't wavered, there's no reason to think that you won't come out of the experience successfully in the end.

It's also worth stating that *your* purpose for enrolling in college and *your* goal for the outcome is unique to **you.** It has to be. After all, it's your education, right? The particular search criteria that you use to select the school you'll eventually attend won't fit anyone else – and as a result, the method to your college search will be unique to you as well. It doesn't matter what your best friend, girlfriend, or boyfriend has planned for his or her own college years - nor does it matter that the girl at the barn with the gorgeous chestnut gelding is rumored to be getting recruitment calls from the head coach at one of the big NCEA equestrian schools. Your college search is yours and yours alone.

Parents, you have dreams and goals for your children too, but as they grow into young adults, their paths might divert from the ones you hoped they'd follow when they were small children. In order for your child to be truly successful at the college level, you'll have to accept the journey they take, even as it changes from its original course. You and the entire family can go on the search together, but in the end, the one who truly owns the school decision is the student - which is why it's important to build a list of potential schools based the priorities that are most important in *the student's* life.

Perhaps that research list will contain the names of some schools that friends and relatives have never heard of or schools that aren't as "selective" or "impressive" as some of the other ones that you hear discussed in your office or in the stands at the horse show. Students, you might not hear classmates refer to the schools that you're interested in as a part of their own college conversations, but that doesn't mean that you've assembled a list of bad schools or that your future college will be any less prestigious than the ones that are part of our collective college vernacular (the Harvards and Yales of the world). It means that you have taken full control of your own college search and have chosen schools that match your own interests and needs rather than following popular trends.

For those who aspire to become professional horsemen (or women), however, the college question can be even more confusing. If you fall into this category, perhaps you wonder if four years of college will be a waste of time that could be better spent in the saddle or working in a barn to gain experience and make professional contacts. Or perhaps you'd prefer to go to a college with an equine major or minor program in the hopes you can gain some additional skills before you join the ranks of the other professionals. Either way, you might just be overwhelmed with the whole process and feel that there's too much pressure on you to make such a big decision within too short a time period:

Do you **have** to go to college? If you don't go, will that ruin the rest of your life?

The short answer for all high school students (unfortunately) is that there *is* no straightforward answer to that question. A 2013 examination of Labor Department statistics by the Economic Policy Institute discovered that those Americans who had four-year college degrees earned ninety-eight percent *more* per hour than those who didn't have degrees. This number was up a full eighty-nine percent from data compiled in 2008. Also, a slightly older study from 2004 learned that women who graduated from college earned (on average) 76 percent more than those who did not. So while those numbers certainly seem to indicate that a college degree is a worthwhile investment of your time and money, statistics aren't everything. You should examine additional factors that are personal to you, including:

- **The financial cost of earning your degree.** In 2012, the average college student graduated with loan debt of $29,400, just over a one percent increase from the year before (but an increase nonetheless). For a student who will work in a high-earning field, loan debt will be less of a factor after graduation than it will be for a student who plans to take a job with less earning potential. (Also bear in mind that many careers require a graduate or professional degree and the above figure only calculates undergraduate debt. Some careers – medical, law, and even education-related - may put you into deeper debt before you're able to begin earning a salary to pay it off.)

- **The time spent to earn your degree.** A 2011 survey from the National Center for Education Statistics found that the only 59 percent of students who enrolled at a four-year college or university were able to complete their degrees within six years. (Notice that figure was *six* years of school, not four.) There are many colleges in the U.S. that have very high four-year graduation rates, but there are others where you will need to commit five or six years to getting your bachelor's degree so that you can complete the necessary coursework. As a result, before you enroll, examine your goals and the schools that are on your list to see what kind of time commitment will be required for you to earn that degree.

- **Your learning style.** Do you love to read? Are you the type of person who enjoys school and can learn things through a combination of classroom lectures and discussions? College classes will require you to read and retain more information than those you're taking in high school and often you'll be assessed by your professors in the form of research papers and essays that require you to demonstrate the depth of your knowledge on the topic assigned. Your courses will be taught in a classroom much the same way you are in high school - only on a larger and more demanding scale. If this type of learning doesn't appeal to you but you still want a college degree, perhaps an accredited online degree program will be a good fit, as it will enable you to work somewhat at your own pace without the distractions of a classroom. Or maybe you're more suited to hands-on, experiential learning – if so, a traditional college education may not be a good choice for your learning style, but perhaps a skilled trade program will be a better choice.
- **Your goals.** The goals you have for your future will have the biggest influence over your need for a college education – as well as what type of degree or certificate you should pursue. Since you can't be a doctor or lawyer without multiple degrees, if those career goals are on your list, you'll need to start your educational journey as an undergraduate seeking a Bachelor's degree. Likewise, most white collar jobs require at least a four-year degree for new hires, but there are other options that require some college but not a full Bachelor's degree, including:
  - *Veterinary technician, dental hygienist, web designer, paralegal.* A two-year associate's degree can be enough to get you hired into one of these fields.
  - *Horse trainer.* There is no prescribed pathway to this career. A two- or four-year degree in anything from biology to accounting or even psychology can be extremely helpful – or you can open your barn with no formal college degree at all. There

are American certification programs through organizations like the USHJA and USDF, as well as programs such as the Certified Horsemanship Association to help you hone your skills and also international certification programs available - such as the British Horse Society program, in which you can earn an international trainer's passport that would make you employable in different countries around the world, not just the United States.

Regardless of whether or not you decide to pursue a college degree, most advisors from a variety of industries can agree that **everyone** in **every** career field should pursue some form of education if they want to be successful. The things you have learned in your four years of high school and eighteen years of living are a wonderful jumping off point as you move into adulthood, but you're not a finished product yet. You owe it to yourself to commit to your personal education whether it arrives pre-packaged in the form of a college degree or in another manner.

If you hope to become a horse trainer or manage a barn, it's worth noting that the career of a professional equestrian is one of the most physically and mentally demanding fields you will find. Not only do they work long hours with the greatest of responsibilities to the well-being of their horses and clients, but they must be educated in a host of innumerable topics, including riding, veterinary science, equine anatomy and physiology, agriculture, business and accounting, psychology (human *and* equine), physics, agriculture, and even fields like geology and meteorology. Those are a lot of different subjects to become well-versed in and you could spend years getting the multiple degrees that it would take to become an expert in each field if you wanted!

Of course, you also have the option to earn a degree that is specific to the equine field too. Because it's a widely held belief in the United States that a college degree is the gold standard in education, many aspiring equine professionals get caught in the middle of the "college" versus "no college" debate simply because they wish to give themselves as much credibility in the marketplace as they can as an educated horse person – and educated person in general. The best thing *you* can do if you fall within this category is to answer the "college or not" question based on the goals that you have set for yourself - ask yourself where your weak areas are and what type or form of education will help to strengthen them. Are you strong on the riding side of things but in need of a more thorough knowledge of stable management? Do you find veterinary science fascinating and want to learn as much as you can so you can keep your horses as healthy as possible? Are you really talented when it comes to communicating with horses but lack in good communication skills when it comes to their owners and/or potential sponsors? Do you understand how marketing and accounting work for small businesses or would a traditional business degree be useful for you in that area?

One other point of consideration for each aspiring future professional horseman is this: Working with horses as a trainer and stable manager and working as a riding instructor doesn't *just* entail working with horses every day. Every horse sent to you for training or sale comes with at least one person attached to it – and probably more! The majority of your clients will probably be amateur and junior horse owners and riders who will come to you from a wide variety of backgrounds, belief systems, and educational histories. You'll also work with a host of veterinarians, farriers, fellow trainers, judges, feed dealers, tack store owners, and potential sponsors – to say nothing of the staff that you may have working under you. To each one of them, you could potentially be a teacher, a therapist, a manager, a bookkeeper, a boss, an employee, a communication and public relations expert, a scientist, a farmer, a client – and quite possibly you will be a combination of all of those things! A college degree in nearly any subject area might just be the thing to help you understand how best to serve each of your clients, vendors, and staff members one day – and the horses themselves might turn out to be the easiest part of the equation!

Finally, if you're truly undecided as to how college can help you as an aspiring professional equestrian, perhaps you and your parents should discuss the idea of a gap year. Though once thought to be only an option for students coming out of school systems in the United Kingdom or for the extremely wealthy, gap years are becoming increasingly popular for more traditional students within the United States as they begin to see the value of gaining hands-on experience in a particular area before entering college. For someone who hopes to enter the equine industry, a gap year can offer the opportunity to immerse yourself in the day-to-day operations of a busy equestrian facility for a full 365 days so you can not only determine whether it's a career path you would like to pursue, but also discover firsthand what gaps in your current knowledge need filling – all while you increase your skills and experience.

Should you decide that a gap year to become a working student is the right choice for you before you enter college, you'll need to sit down with both your parents and your current trainer to work out a formal plan for your year; after all, a gap year is not a vacation where you can sleep late and ride whenever you want to. Instead, you'll need to find an appropriate situation – ideally with a trainer who isn't your regular one so that you can learn new methods and work with someone who can offer a new point of view and fresh experiences. The most important thing is that you should be safely challenged and have opportunities to learn each day. Your trainer should be able to help you in the selection process by identifying horsemen or women who will be a good fit to supervise you. You'll also need to determine who will fund your expenses during your gap year; will your parents chip in or will you be required to pay for everything by yourself? Will you continue to live at home or will you need to find an apartment near the barn? Will you keep your horse or sell him? Will competition be part of your schedule or will it simply be a year spent behind the scenes? The answers to all of those questions must be researched and answered before you can commit yourself to your year of learning.

Also remember that a gap year is just that: a one year *gap* between two traditional educational settings (high school and college) or between high school and working in the real world. At the end of your gap year, you'll need to have a firm plan for college in place if you intend to enroll and must take the appropriate steps to ensure that you have a place on campus in the fall. In many instances, you will apply (and be accepted) to colleges during your senior year of high school and select your chosen school before high school graduation alongside the rest of your classmates. You will then defer your enrollment for the one-year period of your gap. There is normally a required enrollment deposit in order for your spot to be saved, as well as some additional paperwork, but the process can be quite straightforward in many cases. Not all schools will save your place, however, and you may need to reapply to your first choice college during your gap year period if you wish to enroll when you've completed your working student position. Also, financial aid paperwork will need to be completed in both years so that updates or changes in financial situation can be appropriately reported to the college's financial aid office. (The aid offered to you prior to your gap year may not be guaranteed for the following year when you enroll; you will have to consult directly with the college's financial aid office to determine if this will be the case or not.)

Remember students, no matter what form it takes, a college education not only shapes you academically and socially, but it teaches you how to think as you move into your future. For many of you, college will be the first time you live away from home – it may even be the first time you leave your home state. Both the lessons learned inside *and* outside of the classroom will stick with you for the rest of your life - yet a college education as a whole can take many different forms and there is no singular, prescribed path that every student must follow. (Being an equestrian doesn't even differentiate you when it comes to college search confusion – there are basketball and soccer players who might seem to have it all figured out by senior year, but chances are that when it comes right down to it, they're just as confused and uncertain as you are.)

After high school graduation, the choice regarding your educational future will be all yours (though it's a safe bet to say that your family will most likely have a lot of input). But if you decide to pursue a college degree, you have the option to sit in a classroom on a traditional campus with ivy-covered brick buildings or take classes online from the comfort of your own kitchen table or home office. You can educate yourself through a gap year spent as a working student at a show jumping farm in Wellington or spend a year spent volunteering for a mission in South America to learn more about the world outside your community. No matter what you choose to do, though, make sure that you do so with a firm purpose behind your actions. The most important thing is to seize the opportunity after high school to learn as much as you can about those subjects that you're most passionate about and then use what you learn to set up the type of future that you want for yourself.

2

I WON'T GO TO COLLEGE IF I CAN'T RIDE

"I think it's great for prospect[ive] students who are weary of managing barn time with school time to understand that riding at school, although it takes up time and energy, can sometimes be a sort of rejuvenating experience that is very worthwhile for many reasons." **Ruthie, IHSA hunt seat and IDA dressage alumna**

As a dedicated high school equestrian, there's a distinct possibility that the reason you decided to read this book is because it has the words "horses" and "equestrian" in the title. Most likely all of the other college books that your parents and teachers suggested to you *didn't* reference riding so this one is a compromise for all of you. In fact, this might even be the only college book you'll read before you make your campus visits and send applications. The reason? This is a book that understands your passion for the sport and will help you to continue to participate after high school.

Parents, if you're reading alongside your son or daughter (or perhaps stole it when they weren't looking), there's a chance that the only reason you purchased this book in the first place was because it had "college" in the title next to the word "equestrian" and - like most parents in your situation - you are well aware that the only way your child will happily read a book about finding a college is if it also prominently features horses. (The compromise obviously works both ways.)

Whether you are a student or a parent, take a moment to think: What types of conversations has your family already had about college? Have you discussed the pros and cons of obtaining a college education, the sorts of opportunities that are available to college students, and what career options await college graduates? Or has your college conversation begun and ended with in conflict the very moment that riding as part of one's college education and college experience come up?

Parents, think back to your own college days if you attended: How did you make friends? Where did you meet people who weren't your roommate? What sorts of people did you gravitate toward on campus?

Just as with any other transitional experience, when students leave home for college, they leave familiar surroundings, the protective cocoon of the people they've known, and routines they've established since childhood. It's a transition that is filled with uncertainty and a lot of "firsts" – enough to fill a student with anxiety. For most, college is the first time he or she will share space with a roommate, the first time he or she is solely responsible for getting to class (and meals) on a regular schedule, and many other similar experiences. Between the establishment of new routines and all of the new and unfamiliar faces your student will encounter on campus, doesn't it make sense that he or she will choose to go to a new place where there is a high degree of probability that many of those new people will be horse people? That shared interest can create an immediate and comfortable bond amidst all of the other uncertainty.

A cautionary word to students, however: Before you choose that perfect (and, yes, appropriately horse-oriented) college, you must first know what your own personal definition of an "equestrian college" *is*. Is it somewhere that will welcome both you and your horse into the on-campus equestrian center? Is it a place where your class schedule will be flexible enough for you to continue to compete at the big indoor horse shows scattered across the fall calendar? Is it somewhere that boasts a large IHSA team of which you can become a part? Or is it something completely different?

College equestrian programs and intercollegiate equestrian teams come in all shapes, sizes, forms, and personalities and the term "equestrian college" only begins to scratch the surface of the opportunities available to you. As a result, it will save a lot of time (and money too) if you begin the hunt with an educated eye as to what options you will encounter along the way and which ones will work best for you in the end.

(**Author's Note**: During your research, you will probably discover that there are several college riding organizations that align with your riding history and interests, so you won't necessarily have to limit your search to just one type of school or riding program. Also, don't rule out using college as an opportunity to expand your equestrian horizons – maybe there's a new discipline you'd like to try if the opportunity presents itself. Many a hunter rider has traded her Tailored Sportsmans for some western bling while in college and had a wonderful time doing it!)

This chapter will give a brief overview of the various equestrian organizations that are currently available to college students in the United States (and some parts of Canada) and outline its structure and competition format. Parents and students, it can be helpful for you to discuss the options together (especially in regard to your current equestrian participation) before you begin the college search so that you know early on what types of programming you are looking for and can begin to focus on schools that feature those options.

The current organizations are:

- **The Intercollegiate Horse Show Association (IHSA).** Founded in 1967 by then-college student Bob Cacchione, the IHSA is the oldest and largest of the intercollegiate equestrian groups. Spanning the United States and even reaching into Canada, the IHSA currently has a presence at over 370 colleges and universities and is a co-ed sport.

  (**Author's Note:** Some colleges also recognize it as part of their varsity athletic offerings.)

  Riders can compete in either hunt seat (on the flat and over fences) or western (horsemanship and reining) and at some schools are allowed to participate in both. (Hunt seat and western meets, however, are usually held independently from each other.) The format of the IHSA is simple: Each school that hosts a show (or "meet") is responsible for providing all of the horses that will be used in the competition. Riders from the visiting schools need only show up with their show attire and a coach or designated school representative.

Each team must carry a roster of riders with varying experience levels if they want to be successful as well – eight separate levels (from beginner walk-trot through Medal/Maclay) are offered for hunt seat riders and six levels (beginner walk-trot through Open/Reining) are offered for western. (In fact, most coaches will say that their hardest level to fill is always beginner. Countless non-riding roommates have been introduced to the sport this way!)

IHSA riders draw their mounts from a pool of horses provided by the host school before each class. They mount and go before the judges without any chance to get to know the horse first. (All horses are warmed up by non-competing riders prior to the start of the show.) Judging is therefore entirely based on the skills of each rider in the class, not on the talents of the horse. Points are awarded as the classes are placed (seven points for first place, five for second, etc.)

- **The National Collegiate Equestrian Association (NCEA).** Formerly known as NCAA equestrian, the team format for NCEA-member equestrian teams is the only one that is run under the rules and guidelines of the National College Athletic Association (NCAA), which recognizes equestrian as one of its "emerging" sports. NCEA teams are restricted to female athletes only and are be found at schools within NCAA Divisions I and II, but not NCAA Division III. Currently, there are twenty-two NCEA teams in the United States; there are none in Canada.

Like the IHSA, NCEA equestrians compete in the disciplines of hunt seat (on the flat and over fences) and western (horsemanship and reining). The format of the NCEA is also similar to the IHSA in that the host school provides the mounts that all riders will compete on. *Unlike* the IHSA, however, all meets are held in head-to-head format, with only two schools competing against each other at one time. Second, the horse draw is structured so that one rider from Team A will ride off against one rider from Team B; both will ride the same horse in the same pattern or over the same course and the point will be awarded to the rider whom the judges decide has ridden that particular horse better. Riders are also allotted four minutes of warm up with their horses prior to their ride. (For reiners, five minutes are allotted). For the flat portion of the hunt seat competition, a "test" (similar to dressage) is ridden and can require movements like shoulder-in and even ask the riders to drop their stirrups. There is no beginner division for NCEA riders.

(**Author's Note:** The NCEA recruitment process is more thoroughly outlined in Chapter Seven of this book.)

- **The Intercollegiate Dressage Association (IDA).** One of the newer college equestrian organizations, the IDA was founded in 1995 so that dressage riders would have an outlet for competition similar to their hunt seat and western peers. IDA member riders can be found at just over fifty colleges in the United States and Canada and compete in four separate levels from Introductory (walk-trot) through First Level (advanced). The organization is co-ed and – similar to the IHSA and NCEA – host schools are responsible for providing the horses that are used at each meet.

The primary difference between the horse draw for an IHSA/NCEA meet and an IDA show is that IDA teams draw *groups* of horses (one group of four horses per team of four riders) and coaches then assign one horse to one rider from the group. The selection of a particular group of horses is random but the individual rides within the team are at the discretion of the coach.

IDA meets are run very similar to United States Dressage Federation (USDF) horse shows; the arenas and markers used are the same and the tests are Introductory, Training Level, and First Level tests taken directly from the USDF test book for the current competition year. Riders are allotted a ten minute warm up period on the horse that their coach has selected for them and, during the warm up, the coach is allowed to offer tips and pointers. At the end of ten minutes, the rider must stop his or her warm up and proceed to the competition arena. When the judge rings the bell, he or she performs the required test and is scored the same as would be found at any USDF-recognized competition, including all coefficient movements except the coefficient mark for gaits. When the class is placed, points are awarded to the competing riders based on the order of finish (seven points for first, five points for second, etc.).

- **The American National Riding Commission (ANRC).** With just over 70 participating colleges and universities in the United States, the ANRC is another growing college equestrian organization that offers opportunities for intercollegiate competition. An affiliate of the United States Equestrian Federation (USEF) and United States Hunter Jumper Association (USHJA), the organization seeks to educate young riders (both men and women) in the American system of forward seat riding.

Shows consist of two divisions of competition – novice level (for riders jumping two feet six inches) and national level (for riders jumping three feet). The teams that represent their schools in competition are normally small (four riders to a team) and each team is required to bring their own horses with them. (Students are allowed to use their own or may borrow or lease them from their school or coach.)

The competitions consist of four parts: a program ride (equitation on the flat), a derby phase (a hunter trial type outdoor course in with traditional hunter fences), a medal phase (a USEF medal-type course within an arena), and a written phase (with questions pertaining to forward riding theory and horse management). Riders who compete successfully not only have the opportunity to help their team to victory, but may also earn their ANRC certification from the USHJA.

- **The United States Polo Association (USPA).** The USPA's intercollegiate division can be found at nearly sixty colleges and universities in the United States and Canada. Men's and women's teams are allowed and all matches must be played under standard USPA arena rules (which means that all matches are held indoors). Similar to other college equestrian organizations, the home team at a college polo match provides all of the horses to be used in the match. (Substitutions are allowed where necessary during play.)

One difference from the other equestrian organizations, however, is that the two competing polo teams share strings of horses between them. That is, in the third chukker, Team A will ride the same horses that Team B played in the first chukker and vice versa. This (ideally) levels the playing field for both teams during the course of the match and allows horses a full chukker for a rest period. Matches are scored under traditional USPA arena scoring rules.

- **The National Intercollegiate Rodeo Association (NIRA).** Not limited to just horsemen and women, the NIRA was founded in 1949 and today can be found at nearly 140 colleges and universities in the U.S. Co-ed teams compete in the areas of saddle bronc and bareback riding, bull riding, calf roping, steer wrestling, team roping, barrel racing, tie-down roping, breakaway roping, and goat tying. (Four of the events are designated for the women; six are designated for men.)

The rodeo team members who compete in events that require a specially-trained (non-bucking) horse (e.g. steer wrestling, roping, barrel racing, etc.) are required to take their own horse (or horses) and equipment to college rodeo events. Competitors are likewise responsible for transporting the animals themselves. Only the stock (bucking animals and animals used in the roping events such as steers, goats, and calves) are provided by the host college or university.

- **The Intercollegiate Eventing League (IEL).** Formerly known as the West Coast Collegiate Eventing League (WCCEL), this program was founded by students at the University of California-Davis in 2009 in the hope that eventing students from other nearby (West Coast) colleges would have an interest in competing against them in a team format. In 2013, a partnership between UC Davis and Clemson University expanded the organization to cover more of the United States. It was at this time that the IEL was formalized.

In order to gain as many participants as possible, the IEL is open to both men and women and riders participate in teams of three or four. If there are individual riders from different schools present at a competition, they are allowed to compete together as a scratch team. In addition, riders need not all compete at the same level; the scoring system in the IEL accounts for different levels to allow them to participate on the same team. Riders in the IEL must bring their own horses to competitions and are responsible for transporting them. (As with other collegiate equestrian organizations, students who don't own horses are allowed to compete on borrowed or leased mounts if they wish.) An annual Collegiate Eventing Team Challenge is held annually and is specifically geared to IEL member teams; other collegiate eventing competitions are currently held in conjunction with United States Eventing Association (USEA) events and horse trials and the program continues to grow and expand each year.

- **The Intercollegiate Saddle Seat Riding Association (ISSRA).** The ISSRA was founded in 2008 by Dr. Sally Haydon of Lexington, Kentucky at the urging of college students from several schools within the Lexington region. Currently, there are approximately twelve participating colleges and universities who hold membership in the organization. Similar to the IHSA and IDA, riders in the ISSRA range from skill levels of beginner (walk-trot) to advanced (open equitation) and the sport is co-educational. The schools that host the meets are responsible for providing horses for all participating riders to draw at random. One minute of warm up time is allowed to each rider before he or she rides for the judge(s). Points are awarded as the class is placed (similar to the IHSA and IDA), not in a head-to-head format (as in the NCEA).

- **The AQHA Collegiate Horse Judging Contest.** For horsemen and women who prefer not to ride but still have an interest in all things horse-related, the American Quarter Horse Association (AQHA) holds an annual collegiate horse judging contest at its World Championship Show in Oklahoma City, Oklahoma, as well as one at their All-American Quarter Horse Congress in Columbus, Ohio. Students must be current AQHA members in order to participate and any students who come from schools where there is not enough interest to form a full team may compete as individuals if they would like to. As an added bonus, the competitors have an opportunity to earn equine-specific scholarships for their respective schools.

AQHA horse judging teams are normally made up of four or five students and they judge four halter (conformation) classes and eight performance classes, each with four horses in them. (Performance classes can range from western pleasure to hunter under saddle to trail or even pleasure driving.) Students watch, judge and place the classes as they see fit, then give detailed reasons for the decisions they've made to a panel of registered AQHA judges who score their results. (Reasons must be given orally.) Eight hundred points are possible for the competition, half of which are based on the student's placing of each class and the other half of which are based on the strength of the reasons they give for their decisions.

- **The Association Internationale des Etudiants Cavaliers (AIEC).** Supported by the Federation Equestrian Internationale (FEI) and governed by student riders worldwide, the AIEC is not only set up to encourage and support international equestrian competition, but also heavily emphasizes the ideals of cultural exchange. Home countries organize not only horse shows (wherein all horses are provided to the competing students by the host country/school), but also plan social events for all student competitors to attend during their time in the host country. Competitions have been held worldwide over the years, but most of them occur within western Europe and in Canada. The competition focuses on the disciplines of dressage and show jumping and is run in a World Cup format; dressage riders must be riding at FEI Prix St. George level or above and show jumpers must be competing at 1.3 or 1.4 meters in order to qualify. Team and individual competition is offered and membership is open to any college or university student from any country who attends the annual general assembly meeting.

- **The United States Pony Club (USPC).** Though technically not a *college* equestrian organization, a fairly recent change in the age rules for USPC participation allows riders to remain (or become) youth members until they reach twenty-five years of age. Riders must join through a local USPC riding club or riding center but do not have to own their own horse in order to participate. Both men and women are allowed to be members.

The mission of the USPC (as stated on their web site) is to "develop character, leadership, confidence and a sense of community in youth through a program that teaches the care of horses and ponies, riding and mounted sports." The main idea is that riding in competition is but one facet of being a horseman or woman and that stable management, understanding of the history and development of equestrian sport, and the ability to work as part of a team (and do so safely) is equally - if not more - important in equestrian sport.

USPC members ride and compete in a variety of disciplines from dressage, to three-day eventing, show jumping, and mounted games like polocrosse and gymkhana. Some competitions are held in team format and others are for individuals. In addition, the USPC has a rating system wherein students can be examined on their riding abilities and their horse knowledge and achieve different ratings based on their current skill level with D-level being the lowest and A-level the highest.

Do any of these organizations sound like the type of experience you're looking for as a college equestrian? Are you ready to go online and learn more about them, then research what schools offer such programming?

Perhaps you're well on your way to joining one of the teams described previously, but there's always a chance that you could remain unsure. For those of you in the undecided camp, remember, you don't have to join a formal intercollegiate equestrian team in order to continue riding in college. There's nothing wrong with the decision to continue to work with your own horse and your home trainer or another trainer who is located near your chosen college campus if you have personal goals that you wish to achieve during your college years. Or maybe you and your parents think it will be best if your trainer keeps your horse at his or her barn so that you can travel to meet the barn at shows or for lessons over weekends and break periods. There are no truly "bad" options for you to explore; you're working from a relatively clean slate as you prepare to make the transition.

With that in mind, you also can't say that you have truly exhausted *all* of your college riding options until you and your parents discuss the option of putting your riding career on hiatus while you're earning your degree. While the idea of not riding is certainly no one's favorite topic (least of all yours), it's not out of the realm of possibility for you to take a break during your undergraduate years. Academic commitments and outside activities in college utilize your time differently than they do in high school and riding itself has a way of consuming large amounts of time whether you're involved in required practice sessions for an intercollegiate team or simply taking lessons to advance your own personal goals. As such, if you look ahead, take a moment to realize that, if you remove one very time-consuming activity from your life (riding), you will suddenly be in possession of more available hours which can then be filled with classes and homework, as well as with new interests that you might discover as a college student. Perhaps you're interested in doing volunteer work or traveling abroad or doing several internships to discover your dream career; college is meant to be a time of self-discovery and a chance to try things that you might otherwise not and perhaps it can be an opportunity for you to discover what life is like outside of riding.

Think back: Have you never had a period of time in your life when you didn't ride - even briefly? If you answered "no" and have never experienced life without horses and that daily pilgrimage to the barn, perhaps taking some time away from the sport will show you that there are other activities you love just as much – or conversely, you may only last one semester before you hurry back to the barn and swing your leg over a horse again!

No matter what route you choose for your college equestrian career, however, the most important thing you can do to prepare yourself is to sit down with your parents and maybe even with your current trainer to examine *all* of your options for riding (including the unfavorable option of not riding) during your college years. Make pro and con lists for each possibility and then – only after careful examination - make a decision. And whatever decision that is, make sure to choose the path that will help you learn the most new things and make a host of new friends along the way. In fact, the very best reason to select the particular path that you wish to follow will be because you examine all of the others available to you and realize that you can't picture yourself doing anything else!

3
UNDERSTANDING LIFE AS A COLLEGE EQUESTRIAN

"I met some of my lifelong friends through the equestrian program [in college] and I will be forever thankful for that. The shared interest helped develop bonds that are unparalleled compared to friends I have made in other settings."
Lauren, IHSA hunt seat alumna

The previous chapter featured an overview of the different types of college equestrian organizations that are available to you after high school, but as you begin to surf the Internet and visit the web sites of various college riding programs and teams, you'll no doubt encounter a variety of new terms that all *seem* to refer to the same thing at first glance, but upon closer examination turn out to be completely different. In addition, while you may believe that you have a good idea which of the college equestrian organizations most interest you or would be a good fit for your riding background and skills, there is also probably a part of you that wonders if you'll be able to "cut it" if you follow that route. How will you stack up against your peers as a potential new teammate? What types of things should (or shouldn't) you do as you approach tryouts for the riding team? What's the best strategy to help you get ahead of the game?

In order to enhance your understanding of the world of intercollegiate equestrian competition beyond basic descriptions of the organizations themselves, this chapter will give an overview of the common terminology you will encounter as you investigate different types of programs. It will also outline some of the ways in which you can set yourself up as a strong candidate for any team you decide you'd like to join.

When it comes to intercollegiate equestrian vocabulary terms, the most commonly used (and misunderstood) word is **varsity.**

If you haven't seen it yet, the more you examine intercollegiate programs, the more you will no doubt run across programs that are described as **varsity.** All of the NCAA-sanctioned teams that compete within the NCEA carry the **varsity** distinction because of their affiliation with the NCAA, which governs **varsity** sports at many of the colleges and universities in the United States. NCEA riders are therefore listed on the varsity team web sites of their home schools alongside their fellow athletes from football, track, and the rest of the university's athletic offerings.

Yet as you continue your research, you'll most likely discover that some of the IHSA teams you encounter are labeled **varsity** *too* and likewise are featured on their school's athletic web sites. In fact, if your search is particularly thorough, you may even come across a varsity dressage or rodeo team at some point and begin to wonder what makes a team "varsity" in the first place!

In the simplest of terms, a **varsity** team is considered to be one of the principal sports that represent its college or university in athletic competition. **Varsity** sports earn this distinction when a school chooses to support the team financially in return for the students on the team maintaining a certain academic standard as well as a standard of good moral conduct both in athletic competition and in the classroom. By supporting these student athletes, the college or university administration hopes that the accomplishments of the team will help develop and enhance the school's image and that, as a result, prospective new students will be encouraged to apply and enroll and donors will be encouraged to support the school's development efforts. Support of athletic teams also allows colleges and universities to practice the philosophical ideal of "mens sana sit in corpore sano" or "a sound mind in a sound body;" that is, to understand that the education of the mind goes hand in hand with the education of the body.

Varsity athletic teams are *not* required to award athletic scholarship money to their members (though many do). But regardless of which players receive scholarships to assist with the cost of college attendance, each member of a **varsity** team has the school's full financial backing when it comes to playing his or her sport.

(**Author's Note:** All scholarships – including, but not limited to athletic, academic, and riding awards - will be more fully addressed in Chapter Nine of this book.)

The college or university athletic budget covers the cost of the coach's salary, maintenance of the athletic facilities (from playing fields to locker rooms), uniforms for all team members, transportation to and from athletic contests, and all other costs associated with training and competition for the **varsity** teams (including entry fees, etc.). Players generally do not have to pay for anything associated with their sport - though some smaller colleges with minimal athletic budgets often require that their varsity teams participate in one substantial fundraising event each year to help offset some of the costs that aren't covered within the budget itself.

As your search expands, you will undoubtedly discover that **varsity** equestrian teams are quite common in several regions of the United States but are less common in others. In the regions that host a wealth of **varsity** equestrian teams and therefore have a lot of student participation in the sport, you will sometimes run across schools that have **junior varsity** equestrian teams in addition to their **varsity** groups. As with most organizations, **junior varsity** riders are there to learn the ropes and solidify their skills before joining the **varsity** group (similar to the way you have seen varsity and JV teams structured in high school sports).

At the college level, participants in **junior varsity** sports normally receive similar benefits to their varsity counterparts in terms of access to coaches, well-maintained facilities, and little or no out of pocket cost to practice and play their sport, but because they are not full-fledged members of the **varsity** squad, they do not get the same amount of opportunities to compete. Instead, they spend the majority of their time practicing in an effort to increase their skills and with the hope of achieving **varsity** status in the future. The **junior varsity** group is also responsible for helping the students on the team who do compete regularly to stay in top form. JV team members may also be called upon to substitute for an injured, ill, or ineligible rider if the situation calls for it.

If an equestrian team is not recognized as a varsity sport by its home college or university, you will most likely find it listed on the general school web site as a **club**, a **club team**, or a **club sport**. Even though there really is no distinction between the three terms and they are often used interchangeably, you will sometimes find **club sports** listed as a segment of the varsity athletics web page while non-athletic **clubs** will be listed as part of the student organizations and activities web page. The main thing that you need to know about **club** teams as a prospective college equestrian is that these types of groups are traditionally student-organized and student-governed and receive either minimal or no financial support from their school in the way that a varsity team does. Instead, these organizations function as part of the other extracurricular (social activity) groups on campus.

Just because these **clubs** don't have the pomp and circumstance (as well as the governance and formal structure) of a varsity athletic team, however, doesn't mean they have to go without school funding. Some schools allow all of their clubs (from canoeing to Quidditch to student government) to request money from a general club fund to help offset the cost of their activities. They will also support and encourage all student activities through assistance with fundraising and publication of news and events – such as putting weekend horse show results in the campus newspaper. Of course, there is no hard and fast rule for club governance and at some schools each **club** is responsible for assuming all of its own costs for activities. These costs must then be paid by the members themselves, either through club-organized fundraisers or directly out of pocket for each individual member.

Because **club** equestrian teams lack the total institutional support of their varsity peers, they usually ride out of local barns with trainers who are located in close proximity to their home campuses. This arrangement means that individual team members are responsible for paying all lesson and transportation fees directly to the trainer or farm. Team members must also make sure that they pay their annual membership fees to the IHSA, IDA, or other sponsoring organization (depending on the type of competitions they participate in), their entry fees at shows, and for purchasing all of their own clothing and equipment.

Before you begin to form the idea that **club** teams are the poorest riders in intercollegiate equestrian sports, however, it should be mentioned that there are many **club** teams currently competing who are so well-established within their campus communities that they organize substantial annual fundraisers to make ends meet – and sometimes even profit. The proceeds from these fundraisers are then able to fund all **club** activities each year so that the members can participate at a reduced cost or even for free. Of course, not *all* **club** teams have such mechanisms in place and instead charge membership dues to the group by year or by semester – funds which pay for the group's equestrian activities and competitions. Finally, there are other **clubs** who provide volunteer labor at their host barn in order to work off lessons and trainer's fees so that they are required only to come up with the necessary funds for competitions while everything else is covered by the work arrangement.

In summary, there are a variety of ways for **club** teams to fund themselves and it's entirely possible that, during your school search, you may encounter four different clubs that are financially structured in four different ways. What's more, no matter how they're funded, you'll probably find that all are successful in intercollegiate competition! The important thing to recognize as you decide which equestrian programs are of interest to you is to keep track of which ones might potentially have a greater financial impact on your college budget each year. Yet don't discount club teams just because of a cost difference – being an integral part of organizing team fundraisers could look great on your resume as you hit the job market after graduation. (It's just the kind of real-world experience and responsibility that many employers are looking for.)

The final term that usually appears when you first begin to

research college equestrian teams – and the one that tends to be the most confusing - is that of a **show team.**

Unlike the fairly clear distinction between varsity and club teams, a **show team** is a more flexible term that tends to have very different meanings for different schools. For some, the **show team** is a segment or extension of the college's equestrian club. The designation is given to the student members who represent their group at intercollegiate competitions. In these situations, the rest of the membership usually fall within the club's social group – they're the ones who might be found volunteering at the local horse rescue or vet clinic or making popcorn for the club's annual horse movie marathon. **Show team** members at these schools also have social memberships to the club, but the distinction differentiates the amount of money that students are required to pay for participation. (Membership dues tend to be higher for those who compete because their activities are more expensive.)

The term **show team** might also refer to a group within a college-run equestrian program that competes in traditional horse shows outside of the intercollegiate offerings. Students who participate on this type of team often own or lease the horses they use for competition and the coaches affiliated with the program or home barn transport them to local or regional shows to represent the college or university in their own individual divisions and events.

To give an example of this type of **show team**, say a college has a group of four talented students that own their own equitation horses and the local "A" show has a medal division for which the coach thinks the four riders are ready. Those four riders can therefore become an independent **show team** to compete under the banner of the school. (Some colleges even help fund this type of showing – perhaps covering transportation and stabling costs for the students and their horses. It's a great way to get their most talented students out in the public eye and recruit new students to join them.)

In the example above, it's important to explain that, though they compete under the "team" organizational structure, students who participate on a **show team** that travels to a traditional horse show compete as individuals. No team placing is given at the conclusion of the show as it is with NCEA or IHSA events. The only **show teams** that are eligible for team placement in a traditional horse show setting are those who compete in a Nations Cup-type event or competitors who participate in the Intercollegiate Eventing League (IEL). (You will recall from Chapter Two that IEL competitions are held in conjunction with regular three-day events and horse trials.)

Regardless of whether the colleges that interest you offer varsity, junior varsity, club equestrian, or are home to show teams, you will better understand what your personal competition options will be as a college equestrian if you begin your search with an idea of where you currently rank in the placement scale for intercollegiate teams. More specifically, you should know what level your experiences qualify you for so that you can begin to see how you will fit into an existing program.

Most of the college equestrian organizations (in particular, the IHSA, IDA, and ISSRA) have in-depth rating and placement systems already in place in order to ensure that riders compete against other riders who share their experience level in the saddle and – more importantly – so that all participants are matched with horses and tasks that they can safely manage. If riders are put into a show situation at the wrong level, it can be construed as cheating or – worse – be dangerous for both human and equine participants.

To determine your particular level (as viewed through the college lens), you must first understand that, within nearly all of the intercollegiate equestrian organizations, your placement into a riding division is based solely on what you have (and have not) done, both in competition and in practice. For hunt seat riders, you'll need a record of what type of shows you have entered, what fence heights you currently school, and what divisions you have competed in (and their fence heights). If you have a background in another riding discipline (dressage, western, eventing, etc.), that will be asked of you as well. For western riders, your placement will be similar; record what type of shows you have participated in (breed organization, 4-H, local open, etc.), how many points you have earned in various riding events (horsemanship, equitation, trail, etc.), and what other disciplines you may have competed in.

If you are one of those lucky riders who grew up on horseback and you've shown up and down the coast at every major competition that fit into your schedule, when you look at the placement forms, you're most likely going to end up in the most advanced division that your prospective intercollegiate organization offers. You will face the most challenging courses and ride more difficult horses than your beginning-level teammates. In contract, because the IHSA, ISSRA, and IDA (for example) both require that teams carry true beginner riders on their rosters, your teammates will only qualify for that division if they have competed very sparingly (or not at all) and have no more than a certain number of weeks of professional riding instruction under their belts. So if you're a prospective team member who took four weeks of riding lessons at summer camp back in middle school, loved it, and now hope to join your college's equestrian team to pursue your interest in horses, you most likely will compete in the beginner (walk-trot) division against riders with a similar amount of experience.

Placements become far less black and white, however, in the mid-section of the roster where riders can have some previous horse show experience in varying degrees. Within this segment of potential riding team members, a coach is allowed some leeway to use his or her discretion in placing riders. The coach can, for example, move a rider *up* one division if that rider's abilities in the saddle are greater than they appear to be on paper. A coach can never move a rider down, however, if they've competed in a division higher than the college coach believes they should safely be at. In that case, the rider will need to stay home and practice until he or she can compete safely in the appropriate division or else join the JV ranks for a semester or year. Riding can be a dangerous sport and paramount in all intercollegiate competition is the well-being of horses and riders; both coach and rider must be certain on the day of the show that the rider can execute everything required at the designated level without harm to horse or rider.

During the period when they are getting to know the newest riders on their team, the majority of IHSA and IDA coaches try to start all of their first-year equestrians out at the lowest level that the placement paperwork will allow them to. This strategy is largely adopted for safety reasons. Later, as they gain competition experience, the scoring system within the IHSA and IDA is designed to move riders up into another level after they accumulate enough points at the lower level – sometimes as quickly as within their first semester or after the student's first year on the team. The pace at which the student advances through the levels depends on the student's abilities and a bit of old-fashioned horse show luck.

For riders who might not have grasped all of the necessary skills to compete successfully at the next level, a coach may choose to hold that student away from shows for a while so that their skills can catch up to the requirements of their competition level. Likewise, if a rider looks as though he or she will "point out" of a lower level too soon, moving into a level for which they are not prepared, it's the coach's responsibility to hold that rider back for a period of time until he or she is ready to move up.

Often, students and their parents are surprised (and dismayed) when a student who has a great deal of riding experience but very little competitive experience is positioned at a low (near beginner) level in their college equestrian debut. In such cases, it's important for both students and parents to realize two things:

First: The choice to keep a strong rider in a lower division is made by the organization's placement form *first.* Because of the way the form is structured, the rider in question would qualify for the same division in college competition at any school he or she chose to attend.

Second: From the coach's point of view, even though the rules allow an advanced rider to move up one division based on ability, the coach will most likely adopt a strategy beneficial to the team by keeping the rider at the low level. In particular, if the team has gaps in the lower divisions or has weaker riders at the bottom, a coach will decide how best to utilize his or her "players" and put them into the position where they will be of the most use to the team's interests. It's really no different than a baseball coach deciding who will play second base and who will play shortstop.

The team concept can be tough to grasp at first if you're new to the college riding format. As a student wrapping up your high school riding career, you're used to relying solely on yourself and your horse in order to win horse shows. When you become a member of a sixteen-person college equestrian team, however, you'll quickly discover that your success or failure isn't solely reliant on what *you* can do, but on what all of you can do *together*. In intercollegiate riding, the goals of the team must always be placed ahead of individuals. The idea can seem counterintuitive after you've grown up participating in traditional horse shows, but it's one of the main ideas at the heart of intercollegiate equestrian competition – and part of what makes it so much fun.

Want further proof that the team format of intercollegiate equestrian competition is unique and that the lower divisions on the team are important?

The last class of the day at both IHSA and IDA competitions is always reserved for the beginners. For IHSA hunt seat and western, this means it's the walk-trot or walk-jog equitation class; for dressage riders, it's the Introductory level test. Many horse shows each year come down to a two- or even three-way tie for winning team at the end of the day - only to have the final decision come down to the results of walk-trot. In fact, at the 2014 Zone Final competition between Rutgers University, Centenary College, and Delaware Valley College – the show that determined which team who would qualify for the IHSA National Championship Show – the decision came down to the walk-trot class at the end of the day. It was the biggest show of the year for all three teams and their fate was determined by the least experienced riders among them! For the advanced riders, all they could do was watch from the rail and cheer on their teammates.

After reading this section and gaining new insight into the structure of intercollegiate equestrian teams, are you now curious about where you would place on a college team?

If you are, it's easy to find IHSA and IDA rider placement forms online. A quick Internet search for the terms "IHSA rider placement form" or "IDA rider placement form" with the current year should be enough to locate one on a school or organization web site. Some of the other organizations' forms are less readily available so you might need to contact a coach or organization representative directly to see if they are willing to share one with you.

Once you find what you're looking for, sit down with your parents or your trainer (or both) and read the information over carefully. Learn what counts within the organizations as a recognized show and what doesn't. Compare your previous competition record and your goals for the coming show season to the divisions outlined on the form. (Prospective IHSA riders take note: the form for hunt seat and for western is the same and there will be overlapping questions so you will need to read everything very carefully.)

It's also important as a prospective college equestrian to make sure you have an accurate count of how many wins you've had in a particular division (hunters, horsemanship, etc.) beginning with your ninth grade year and keep it updated as senior year approaches. Dressage riders, track your highest scores for each level you've shown at both rated and schooling shows, as well as a record of what tests you have ridden (e.g. Training Level Test One versus Training Level Test Three) and how many times you have ridden each one. For hunt seat and dressage riders, web sites such as www.usef.org and www.centerlinescores.com that track scores can help make your search easier. If you're a breed show competitor, track your points in all riding divisions (pleasure, equitation, horsemanship, trail, etc.) on a spreadsheet or other similar form as they accrue; NRHA competitors should track all prize money earned and in what division you participated.

Careful tracking of your competition record will be equally if not more important for you as a prospective equestrian athlete if you're considering joining an NCEA team. Though your initial path will be similar to that of an IHSA or IDA rider, you will also have a great deal of additional paperwork and verification required along the way. The other important step that prospective NCEA riders must take is to register online with the NCAA Eligibility Center at the beginning of junior year. (This makes you eligible for recruitment by coaches.) The online registration form at the NCAA Eligibility Center includes questions about your riding history as well as your academic record (be sure you know when you took each one of your high school courses and how you did in each one – having your high school transcript handy can help), your height and weight, and questions about your family background (parents' occupations, education levels, etc.) There is also a fee charged for NCAA Eligibility registration so you'll need a credit card to sign up. (As previously mentioned, full NCEA recruitment details and additional strategies regarding IHSA and NCEA crossover applications will be discussed in Chapter Seven.)

As Chapter Two explained, there really *is* a college riding option out there for every student who wishes to have an outlet for his or her equestrian interests after high school. This chapter has examined those options a little more in-depth and defined some of the key terms, as well as giving an overview as to the team structure and emphasis at the college level. By now, you should possess a better understanding of what you will encounter as you consider those riding options as part of your overall college search. It is not, however, advisable to base your search for the right college solely on your riding goals; the next two chapters will explain the reasons why.

4

BIG COLLEGES, SMALL COLLEGES, URBAN, RURAL – HOW DO I KNOW WHAT'S BEST FOR ME?

"[My] childhood/ high school experience was not nearly as hectic as my college lifestyle."
Ruthie, IHSA hunt seat and IDA dressage alumna

Just like the variety of college riding options and organized intercollegiate competition opportunities that are available to you after high school, you've no doubt already realized that your school options are just as numerous – perhaps even more so!

What type of school should you apply to?

Should it be big or small?

Would you prefer an urban campus near a thriving city or should it be rural with lots of access to bridle trails?

Should you look on the East Coast or the West - or is there a better school for you somewhere in the middle?

Maybe you should consider only schools close to home in case you want to ride with your home barn during college – or perhaps you should apply to schools of all type, size, and location in order to give yourself several different options when it comes time to make your final decision.

Do the possibilities seem endless? Do you feel as though it would be easier to ride around the four-star cross-country course at Rolex on a green horse than narrow down a list of potential schools that you would love to attend after high school?

You don't need to have the answer to every single question about your school options when you're just beginning to assemble your college list; in fact, you will most likely find that looking at schools of varying sizes that offer different types of programs and are located in different settings will help you determine what sort of school you're looking for in the first place. After all, it's certainly easier to make comparisons in any situation if you have a little bit of everything to choose from at first - you might even discover that you began the search planning to attend a large urban school with ten thousand students and in the end choose to attend a remote liberal arts college with only six hundred!

Many young equestrians begin their college search with an eye toward simplifying the process by only applying to colleges with prominent equestrian programs or equestrian teams – the ones whose names are consistently printed in popular equestrian magazines. **This is a mistake,** not because riding doesn't deserve the appropriate amount of consideration in your decision-making process, but rather because selecting a school based entirely on the equestrian opportunities that you see advertised is a sure way to set yourself up for heartbreak down the line.

For example, you might decide that you'd like to ride on an NCEA team and limit your search solely to those twenty-three schools that ride within that organizational structure. But what if your grades and test scores aren't enough to get you admitted to the universities? Conversely, what if you fall in love with the idea of riding for your favorite NCEA coach, gain admission to the school, and then find out the summer before college begins that the coach has left to work for another school? What if you get a scholarship that expires after your freshman year? Will you be able to pay your tuition and fees without it? Worse yet, what if you become injured and can't ride at all in college?

IHSA and IDA programs aren't immune from disappointing students either; the majority will do team tryouts each fall *after* the start of the academic year. This means that even if you've been admitted to the school and moved into your dorm room on campus, there's often no guarantee that you'll be selected for the team. The

41

largest and most successful teams often have to cut a few riders each fall because they have too many in one division or simply don't have enough funds to support everyone's competitive aspirations. And if club teams have a coaching switch at the last minute or come up short on a fundraising drive, their season can be put into jeopardy as well.

Of course, all of the "what ifs" that coincide with the college search process apply to all students who seek the right college fit, not just equestrians, and there's never a guarantee that anyone can plan ahead for all outcomes. That's the nature of life as much as it is the uncertainty of higher education and intercollegiate athletics. Unfortunately, though, there is enough uncertainty out there that you'll need to base your college decision on more than just your riding opportunities, lest you inadvertently remove some great college possibilities from the table before you've even examined them thoroughly. What's more, you also need to prepare for potential changes that don't even seem possible from where you sit right now – new academic interests, a shift in your riding goals, etc. – so that at the end of the day, you have a balanced list of reasons for why you selected the school that you did (and only one or two of those reasons have anything to do with equestrian sports).

At the same time, you should acknowledge that *not* taking your passion for riding into account as you research potential colleges is the fastest way for you to wind up miserable the moment you set foot on campus. Riding is as much a part of your inner character as it is your outer life and part of the reason that you're a great candidate for college is because of the things you've learned in the barn and in the saddle. This facet of your character is something that you will get to explore and share with others – your parents, other family members, your guidance counselor and teachers, and college admissions counselors – as you embark on your college journey, but it's only one part of you. All of the other parts need to have an equal say into what considerations you take into account during your college search. (The right college fit is all about striking a balance.)

Before you begin to evaluate both your college and college riding options, however, it's important that you have a working understanding of some of the school-related terms you will run across in your research. Just as with the terminology that accompanies the various types of college equestrian organizations that are out there, you'll quickly learn that there are a lot of terms that are used to describe colleges and universities as well – including the words "college" and "university" themselves!

What is the different between a college and a university anyway?

The short answer is that, technically, there is no difference here in the United States and the terms can be used fairly interchangeably. Still, amongst the similarities, there are a few distinctions worth noting. Here are the basics:

A **college** is an educational institution that offers classes and programs toward a degree (such as a bachelor's or an associate's).

Similarly, a **university** is an educational institution that awards degrees to its students. A **university**, however, is made up of various **colleges** that fall under the umbrella of a singular institution.

(In case you're already confused, here's an example: At your local state university, you might discover that there are six or seven different **colleges** listed in the academic catalog. There's a "College of Business," a "College of Engineering," one called "The College of Arts and Sciences," and a few others. All of them are separate programs but they fall under the umbrella of one singular **university**.)

Does that make sense so far?

Here's one more distinction between the two:

Universities are normally dedicated to research in a variety of areas and offer graduate-level degrees, including master's and Ph.Ds. (Medical and dental schools, as well as law schools – all of which are referred to as "professional degrees" - are also to be found at **universities.**)

Next, as your search begins to examine some specific colleges and universities, you'll also notice that there are three different *types* of college and university: public, private, and for-profit.

(**Author's note**: The vast majority of public and private universities fall under the category of not for profit and are recognized by the government as a 501c3, which exempts them from taxes. This is the reason that for-profit colleges fall under their own subheading, as they are required to pay federal taxes annually.)

The next logical question you will ask, then, is probably:

What is the difference between a public, private, or for-profit college or university?

The majority of the schools you will come across in your research will be **public** or **private**, as the number of **for-profit** schools is tiny in comparison.

(Briefly, **for-profit** schools are developed and managed by private organizations or corporations and receive no government funding for their educational efforts. As of July of 2013, approximately twelve percent of American undergraduate students were attending **for-profit** institutions, the majority of whom were working adults, adults with children, and part-time students who were attracted by the flexible scheduling of classes and substantial online class offerings. The University of Phoenix is probably the most well-known **for-profit** school in operation at present.)

As an equestrian looking to pursue your sport at the college level, however, you must understand that riding teams or athletics of any kind are generally not found at for-profit colleges.

As for your other college/university options:

A **public** college or university is one that receives funding (either in large or small amounts) from its state government. At many of the largest **public** universities in the U.S., the majority of those government-allocated dollars are spent on research that is conducted by college or university faculty and students who are at the graduate level. Government support for the institution also means that most **public** schools offer their education at a lower sticker price to their students than **private** schools. (Also, because the state government awards the funds out of taxpayer dollars, students from within the state are asked to pay less than students from out of state.)

As a general guideline (but not a hard and fast rule), **public** universities tend to be larger in both student population and campus size than **private** colleges. The largest concentration of NCAA Division I sports are also found on **public** university campuses and it's those schools who are often recognized by name first for their athletic achievements *and then* for their academic merits.

Conversely, **private** colleges receive their funding from tuition revenue, private donors, and investments. None of their funding comes from their state government. Because many **private** schools have very substantial endowments as a result of these donations and investments, however, they can often offer significant scholarship and financial aid awards to students to help offset tuition that boasts sticker prices higher than those of **public** colleges and universities. (In some cases, students might even discover that a **private** college will cost them less out of pocket than a **public** one because of the availability of this type of funding.) **Private** colleges are often smaller in both student body and campus size than **public** colleges and tend to house NCAA Division II and III athletic teams (though this is not a hard and fast rule either).

Among the private colleges and universities in the United States falls one select group of schools that garner attention each year – a group of schools commonly known as the **Ivy League**.

*(**Author's Note**: The term "Ivy League" was originally coined in the 1930s by journalist Stanley Wood in the *New York Herald Tribune* and most likely was used in reference to the ivy that still

clings to many of the campus buildings).

Today, the **Ivy League** refers to eight private universities in the northeast who share common interests in academics and athletics and are among the oldest in the country. These universities are:

Brown University (Providence, RI)

Columbia University (New York, NY)

Cornell University (Ithaca, NY)

Dartmouth University (Hanover, NH)

Harvard University (Cambridge, MA)

Princeton University (Princeton, NJ)

University of Pennsylvania (Philadelphia, PA)

Yale University (New Haven, CT)

Because they are such a well-established and prestigious set of schools, **Ivy League** universities are among the most difficult schools for high school students to gain admission to each year. (In 2014, Harvard University accepted a mere 5.9 percent of the students who applied.) Students who apply to **Ivy League** schools are among the best and brightest of their year – and even so, the majority of them will wind up at other very good colleges and universities across the nation.

Beyond public, private, and Ivy League colleges, there are also two other types of college you will surely come across in your search: a **liberal arts college** and a **community college**.

A **liberal arts college** is typically a small college with a curriculum that is designed around the development of broad skills that may cross disciplines or academic areas (such as an art class exploring paintings of birds from a scientific and biological perspective). Writing and thinking are emphasized and it's quite common to meet students from **liberal arts colleges** who have combined (double) majors or else have one major and multiple minors on their academic records because the curriculum encourages and allows them to explore divergent interests.

Liberal arts colleges tend to be smaller than other colleges and typically have no graduate programs – though, once more, the rules for this are not ironclad. There's also a better than average chance that the faculty are engaged in independent research alongside their undergraduate students even though the emphasis for faculty members at **liberal arts colleges** is primarily on teaching and mentorship. (Because of this focus, you're unlikely to have a course taught by a teaching assistant at a **liberal arts college**.)

(**Author's Note**: Several **public universities** offer **liberal arts colleges** within their options for majors and courses of study in an effort to give undecided or broadly interested students an opportunity to find this type of education in a more research-oriented environment.)

A **community college** is exactly what it sounds like: it's a college designed to serve the needs of its local citizens and those within its home region or county. The academic programs at a **community college** are designed to grant an associate's degree within a two-year period, so students who wish to obtain a four-year bachelor's degree often use their local community college to begin their college careers and transfer to a four-year school after they've obtained enough credits to do so. Because students can attend a community college for one-third of the cost of a public university or one-tenth of the cost of a private college, this strategy has been adopted by more and more students as tuition prices at four-year schools have continued to climb in recent years.

The **community college** option is also useful for students who want another year or two to improve their study skills or raise their grades before moving on to a bigger school. A **community college** is also a good option for those who have a job near their home that they wish to keep while in school or those who have family obligations that make a more flexible academic schedule more appealing. (The majority of **community colleges'** student bodies consist of commuter students who do not live on campus, though there are many community colleges with residence halls to accommodate distant students or students who want the full college experience of living away from home.)

Finally, if you are a student interested in serving your country in some way after high school, the United States is also home to five different **service academies** that offer a tuition-free education in exchange for five years of military service after graduation and an additional three years in the reserves. (Depending on the post-graduate training required by a particular branch of the service, the term of service may be longer.)

The **service academies** are:

The Air Force Academy (Colorado Springs, CO)

The United States Naval Academy (Annapolis, MD)

The Coast Guard Academy (New London, CT)

The Merchant Marine Academy (Kings Point, NY)

The United States Military Academy (West Point, NY)

Admission to a **service academy** is never a guarantee for any student, however. Top grades in high school and strong test scores on the ACT or SAT are required for consideration, as the schools are among those with the lowest admission rates in the country. In addition, each application must be accompanied by an official nomination from a senator or congressman from your district or from the Vice President or President of the United States. (Nominees to the Coast Guard Academy do not need a nomination; their admission process is direct for top students who meet the requirements.) The senator or congressman from your district will most likely also require that you submit an essay and several letters of recommendation to his or her office before they will make the decision as to whether or not to grant you the official nomination.

Finally, prospective **service academy** students must also be physically fit. Each one must pass a rigorous official physical in order to gain admission and, once admitted, will continue to participate in daily fitness training as part of his or her education.

For prospective college equestrians of all disciplines, it's important that you know that each type of school – colleges, universities, public and private schools, the Ivy League, liberal arts and community colleges, and four of the five service academies – *can* **and** *do* **field equestrian teams.** (As previously stated, the lone exception from the list is for-profit colleges.) From the big to the small, the rural to the urban, if students on any campus in the nation want to ride and compete, they are able to find a way to make it happen – and many of them have the successful show records to prove it!

Are you beginning to see another reason why selecting only those schools with riding teams won't be enough to create a really good college list for you?

With equestrian options available to you across the board, the best place to begin your search is to create a working list that itemizes your other priorities – things such as **cost**, **academic opportunities**, or **location**. These items are the ones you can use as the springboard from which to launch a more effective and targeted search – and they tend to be the easiest ones from which you can begin to compare and contrast what is available to you in the college market.

Don't cast a net that is *too* wide when you examine academics, however. For example, if you want to study biology in college and you begin your search for potential colleges with just a simple web search for "college biology," you'll come up with far more choices than you'll ever have the time to look into.

If you look for colleges that offer biology majors and have equestrian teams that compete in IHSA hunt seat, however, you'll easily weed out some of the schools that won't be a fit for you. (To determine which schools are riding in the IHSA, always consult the "Current Teams" list on their web site, which is updated annually with the names and contact information of all of the schools who are registered to compete during that calendar year.)

To further narrow your search for a college with a biology major and an IHSA hunt seat team, consider location. Do you want to be east of the Mississippi River or west? Do you want to be in a warmer climate or a moderate one? Do you like rural settings or something more urban?

(Just remember as you begin to consider various locations that you're shopping for an educational home for your next four years, not a vacation property with perpetually sunny weather and easy beach access so you can perfect your tan!)

It's not wise this early in the college search to narrow your list *too* far, however, because you don't have enough specific information the individual schools that have made their way onto your list yet. Until you have looked closely at their biology curriculum and alumni outcomes, checked your academic profile against their current freshman class, and seen how their equestrian team is structured and if you think it would mesh with your riding background and goals, you can't truly say that a school works or that it doesn't work.

The very best plan of action is to pay a visit to a college or university that has caught your attention so that you can learn more in person before you decide if it looks and feels like one that you would like to apply to. In fact, you might discover that you lack a list of school names that is long enough after your initial round of searching – it may only be three or four schools to start with and, while it's easy to compare them to one another, it isn't quite a large enough sample to really help you determine what elements will work for you and what might not.

If the initial list is too short, refer to the current list that you have begun and widen your search again – only this time, you can spread a slightly wider net based on the types of colleges that have already piqued your interest. Take a moment to assess *why* you're interested in those first schools and then, in your second search round, use those things that you find appealing to seek out other schools that are similar to them in some way – or even in many ways. (You'll be surprised at how many similar schools you can find if you look hard!)

A good number of schools to have on your list before you begin to schedule campus visits is somewhere around ten – though there is absolutely nothing wrong with a smaller list of six to eight. The most important thing is that, for each school you have an interest in, you have a handful of reasons why each one appeals to you – and remember, only one or two of those reasons can be horse-related.

Once you have a solid list of schools and your reasons for liking them in hand, you're ready to learn more about how you can make yourself a solid candidate for admission and what goes into the process.

5

THE BIG DECISION – WHERE SHOULD I APPLY (AND WILL I GET IN)?

"College is a hard transition and academics should come first. Don't worry about getting to horse shows, or even making a team, because it is so incredibly hard to do everything that you want to do." **Kate, IHSA western alumna**

Every high school student knows the discomfort and dread that accompanies writing a term paper for your AP English class or finishing a big report on World War II that your strict social studies teacher expects to see first thing Monday morning. When you begin, nothing more than a blank page (or blank computer screen) sits before you, practically taunting you with its emptiness and beckoning you to fill it with all the knowledge you can. Yet you know full well that there isn't just one way to write the report or one particular topic that will satisfy the prompt your teacher has used as a tool to get you started. If you want to write the best paper possible and achieve a top grade, you must decide where your strengths lie in the given subject area and then play to them.

Unfortunately, the dreaded "blank page syndrome" and sense of indecision that you feel when it comes time to write that term paper isn't limited to homework. Sitting down to build a list of colleges that interest you can feel much the same when you're first starting out.

What's more, when it comes to your college applications, there won't be a familiar teacher at the end of the process who will pick apart your ideas and offer helpful corrections for improvement. You won't be given an opportunity at a re-write if you want to make a few changes. Instead, when you're done making your list and the applications have all been submitted, a group of complete strangers will determine what path (or paths) will be available to you after you graduate from high school – and that fact alone is enough to make many of you more nervous than you were on the day of your very first horse show.

And, just as on the day of your competitive debut, it won't be enough for you to hear someone tell you to "just relax" and "have fun" because you're weighing a decision that can affect your entire future. It's undeniable and you're absolutely right to regard the situation with the proper amount of seriousness and solemnity as you enter it – but to do so without the proper degree of perspective will likewise cripple your search from the moment it starts.

What kind of perspective should you take to avoid stress? What do you need to know to help ease your fears?

Sometimes it's best to start with some hard numbers. For example: It is a recognized fact in the world of higher education that *eighty percent* of the nearly 4,000 colleges and universities located within the United States accept *eighty percent* of their freshman applicants every year. Eighty percent of 4,000 gives you nearly 3,000 schools to choose from – and eighty percent of those schools is 2,400. That's a lot of colleges to be accepted to! What's more, there are only fifteen colleges in the U.S. who accept less than thirteen percent of their applicants. If you aren't applying to one of those schools, your chances of acceptance can only continue to increase.

If you're a skeptic or a worrier or feel any type of unease about the college application process, however, you might already have thought a step or two beyond getting admitted. In fact, you might be wondering if, after all of the admissions process is done and you've made your final selection, there's a chance you will enroll at your dream school and later discover (after only a semester or two) that it *isn't* your dream school after all.

What then?

Or what if you enroll at that exciting dream school and

discover along the way that your dream has changed? How will you adjust?

The simple answer to those questions is that life is unpredictable. Just as adults often pursue new career opportunities long after earning their first college degrees, the interests and goals of college students are also susceptible to change along the way. (Remember from Chapter One that eighty percent of college students will change their major at least once during their college careers, so there's a very good chance that you'll be among their number.) But college is more than just a bunch of classes that you take and an extension of the same things you've been taught high school. Going to college immerses you in a new place and a new culture; it's designed to help those who don't know what their dream is to discover it and to help those with a firm plan to decide once and for all if it's the correct one for them. If it isn't, they'll need to change course and pursue a different plan – which is another purpose for which college is well suited.

Just as with horses, a college education can often be a bit more malleable than students often give it credit for. How many times have you gone to a show and seen a horse compete in a class, a division, or even a discipline for which it wasn't initially bred? Perhaps you've seen an Arabian that wins jumper classes or a Norwegian Fjord compete at FEI level dressage - or maybe you know an all-around Quarter Horse who has such a willing personality that he excels at everything his rider asks of him. The bottom line is that the riders of those horses don't worry about keeping them in a particular box just because their breeding says they should be there; they evaluate the horse's particular strengths and then send them in that direction. You can do the same with your college search and your eventual college education.

It's also important to remember that when you send your application for admission to potential schools, you do so as a high school senior. That application is therefore nothing more than a representation of who you are and what you've accomplished *right now*. It gives insight into your potential, shows what you're capable of, and reveals to the admissions committee a glimpse of who you will become in the future but it is by no means a demonstration of you as a finished product. As a result, you as a college applicant must choose to submit yourself to schools whose cultures and educational values match your own and schools where you can see yourself developing further during your time there. If you later discover that you aren't happy where you are or that your changing interests and values better align you with a different school, you will be free to transfer to the new school. It really is that simple.

One other common fear that seems to be heavily perpetuated among high school students is that, no matter what schools you apply to, each one will reject you and your only option will be to attend your local community college. This myth of widespread college rejection seems to cast a wider net with every passing year as certain "name brand" colleges continue to publish lower and lower acceptance rates (even though it's usually just those fifteen colleges mentioned earlier in this chapter). In journalism, it's always said that "if it bleeds, it leads," and the bloodbath of annual college rejection is therefore newsworthy – with the stories and social media postings on the subject blown to greater and greater proportion over time. Because news outlets rely heavily on ratings and advertiser dollars, it's in their best interests to perpetuate the biggest headlines that they can, but the unfortunate consequence of it all is that worried parents and students take the information and run with it, causing gossip and rumors to spread like wildfire: Who got in from your high school? Who was deferred? Was anyone denied? "She got *how much* scholarship money?"

What's more, the situation builds and builds until no one really knows what the truth of the matter is anymore. In some particularly competitive high schools, college "shaming" for those who gained acceptance to schools deemed "not good" or "fallback quality" runs rampant and makes matters even worse:

"Did you hear about Susie next door? She was accepted to Stanford but Princeton flat out denied her. Can you believe it? She has perfect grades and test scores! Meanwhile, I know she only got into Cornell because she's a legacy."

Such undermining behavior instantly drains all of the joy and excitement out of the college admissions process for everyone and sometimes even the adults around you – teachers and guidance counselors – aren't immune to its affects. Schools that send their top students to top colleges often have first chance at better and better students to fill their seats in the future, so even as you and your classmates compete for college acceptances, the guidance office is competing against their rival schools. As the atmosphere builds, the situation transitions into one where no longer are you searching for an educational home and a place where you can grow and thrive for four years, but instead you're running an exhausting race to get ahead of everyone around you simply for the sake of wearing a sweatshirt that bears the name of the most prestigious college you can find. Worst of all, it's a race that no one ever really wins.

With all of this tension swirling, is it any wonder that college admission seems like an imposing, scary, and emotionally exhausting process?

Perhaps you and your parents have already experienced parts of this phenomenon. Maybe you've encountered it in the stands at the Friday night football game, on the rail at your local horse show, or in the aisle at your home barn. If you are already in the middle of it, take heart and push your apprehension aside as you memorize this fact:

If the right students are matched with the right schools, they will have many good options for their post-high school years.

You *can* and *will* be admitted to a school that will be a wonderful match for your talents and goals (as well as for your equestrian career) so long as you approach your school list with the proper perspective and conduct thorough, personal research that identifies not only what you *want* in your college home, but also what you *need* if you are to accomplish your goals. In fact, you will find that your school list will largely shape itself if you don't begin with schools at all, but instead begin with an idea of what factors should take priority in your college search.

(**Author's Note**: It's vital to your success that you and your parents make this list of priorities together and that you do so early on in the process – perhaps as soon as sophomore year. This preliminary conversation ensures that you are all very clear about *how* the search will be conducted and helps to prevent miscommunication and misunderstandings that might occur later on.)

The most common elements that play a role in a student's college search are listed below in no particular order. The prioritization of each element must be determined by individual families:

- Cost of attendance
- Proximity to home
- Student population (undergraduate school size)
- Academic programs offered
- Career development opportunities
- Location
- Academic profile/acceptance rate
- Time required to finish a degree
- Student housing options
- Extracurricular programs available
- Athletics (including equestrian sports)
- Campus social life (including Greek life)
- Campus personality/culture

Not all of the listed elements will influence your college list from the moment that you first begin your search, of course. Early on, it's important to take the time to compare schools of varying sizes, locations, and proximity to your home in order to get an initial sense of what appeals to you and what doesn't – and don't make too many assumptions until you've completed some initial research. Just because you attend a large high school doesn't mean that you will only feel comfortable on a large college campus and just because you've grown up in Massachusetts and dislike the winter months doesn't mean that a school in southern California is automatically the right choice There are a lot of nuances to consider and you'll find that you gain a better understanding of yourself and the college search process if you don't gloss over any of them at the beginning.

There are some items, however, that *will* influence your school list from the moment you instigate your research and must be considered all the way through the search. Major items can place significant restrictions on you and the types of schools you're able to consider; for example, if your parents are on a tight budget and the cost of college tuition is going to play a major role in what school you will eventually be able to attend, cost needs to be something you are aware of as you begin to look at schools.

In fact, the cost conversation is one of the most important ones that you and your parents must have in relation to your college search. If your family's financial situation dictates that your education must fall within a certain allowable budget, you have to be careful not to fall in love with schools that are going to be a financial impossibility. When it comes to affording and paying for college, an emotional decision to take on more debt than is reasonable simply for the sake of attending a famous dream school is one that you might find yourself paying for – quite literally – for the rest of your life. (Peer pressure is *never* a good reason to select a school!)

(**Author's Note:** Remember from Chapter Three that the higher sticker price of a private college or university should not automatically exclude that school from your search list if the school has all of the other elements that you seek. Private colleges and universities often use internal funds and discounts to bring their out-of-pocket cost below that of their public counterparts, making them an affordable option for many families.)

It's also important when you discuss a college budget to go beyond a simple discussion of cost and examine the way that your education will be financed in-depth. Will your parents or grandparents cover the full cost of your tuition, room, board, and fees? Will you be required to contribute, either from savings or by getting a job? Do your parents have a budget they have set for you and your siblings that cannot be exceeded? Do you have a college savings account or 529 college plan? Will student loans be considered? And if loans are part of the equation, will they be in your parents' names, your name, or a combination of the two? Who will repay the loans after you graduate – will you pay by yourself or will your parents assist you?

You might not be able to answer all of the questions that go along with paying for your college education right away, but getting them out in the open and reviewing them once makes it far easier to include them in the ongoing college conversation as it deepens over the course of your search.

Also, as you continue to discuss college budgeting for your family, don't forget to take into account tuition increases over your four- to six-year college career. Unless you attend a school with a four-year tuition cost that comes guaranteed (of which there are several in the United States), you'll need to assume an annual increase in costs that ranges anywhere from three to eight percent for each year that you are enrolled. College funding is a multi-year commitment and the best prepared families are those who go in with a plan that spans well beyond the student's first year.

If you're working within a budget for your college expenses and need to know the particulars from a specific college or university, the process of calculating your approximate tuition cost has recently been simplified by a federal government requirement that each school embed a tool called a "net price calculator" into its web site where families can easily access it. Each net price calculator gives a relatively fast estimated figure as to what that individual college might cost *you* in your first year of enrollment. You don't even need to speak to an admissions or financial aid staff member to make it work; all you need is some of your parents' tax information from the current (or previous) year and a list of your most recent grades and test scores. (Some calculators might also ask questions regarding savings accounts, 529 plans, or other related financial information; each calculator runs on an algorithm that is unique to the college or university to which it belongs.) Once you've plugged in the data, the calculator will give you an approximate figure – which, in turn, can show if the school will be a financial feasibility for your family before you send an application for admission.

In addition to the college's own web sites, the government itself has found ways to make college costs more transparent for prospective students. The U.S. Department of Education's student financial aid web site (found online at http://studentaid.ed.gov/) can walk you through not only the basics of financial aid (what types are available and how to apply for it), but also provides a Free Application for Federal Student Aid (FAFSA) Forecaster tool that can help you see what type of government financial aid you might be eligible for – information you can then use to compare to the net price calculator totals you get from the colleges you're interested in.

Finally, should you and your family be considering loan aid to help cover tuition and on-campus living costs, it's very important that you sit down with a financial aid expert or advisor to discuss your options. There are certified financial planners and companies available who work specifically with college-bound students and families to examine all of their funding options for school. Perhaps there is such a company or person in your region whom your family would like to hire to make the process less confusing, but if you cannot afford such support or don't have access to one of these experts, visit the government's loan web site at www.studentloans.gov or schedule an appointment with a financial aid officer at the college or university that you wish to enroll in. He or she will be able to examine your family's ability to pay through the lens of the institution's financial aid awarding policies and walk you through the methods they use to determine what your out of pocket cost will be for that particular school.

(**Author's Note:** Financial aid, scholarships, and student loans will be discussed more completely in Chapter Nine, which focuses on the types of award offers that accepted students might receive and outlines more detailed financial aid strategies.)

Beyond important financial concerns, however, the other element that should heavily influence your college list from the moment you begin to search is your personal academic profile and the academic profile of the schools you're interested in. Here, the term "academic profile" refers to the numbers that appear on your high school transcript - specifically your grades, the types of classes you've taken (in particular Advanced Placement, Honors, International Baccalaureate, etc.), and your test scores (if you've taken the SAT or ACT yet or if you have completed the PSAT or PLAN). If you've never looked at your high school transcript before, sophomore or junior year is a good time to familiarize yourself with what college admissions officers will see when they evaluate your application. Though your school will restrict your access to view your "official" high school transcript (which must be stamped and sealed), it's normally not too difficult to receive a copy of your "unofficial" transcript; just be clear when you or your parents make the request of the counseling office that the version you seek is the *un*official one.

For colleges and universities, the term "academic profile" refers to the academic records and test scores of high school seniors they accepted into their freshman class from the previous year. Some schools will include other information in profile data when it's compiled, such as the number of students who took AP or IB exams, the number of students awarded financial aid, and even the states, regions, and foreign countries where students applied from. The "freshman profile" can be found on the web page of the college's admissions office or on the "About" section of the general school web site. If you can't locate it there, a quick web search for the name of the school and "academic profile" can often help you locate the basic overview you're looking for – though be sure that you select a link to a reputable college site with verified information as opposed to an opinion site with an open forum where students and other outsiders are allowed to share unsupported data.

There's also a good chance that your high school has access to Naviance or another similar program with college data that can help you retrieve not only the academic profile information of schools that are of interest you, but can also show you the academic profiles of previous students from your school that were accepted and have enrolled there. This can be a useful tool to help you see how rigorous a particular college's admission process may be and how you compare to students who share your academic history.

As you examine your personal profile and compare it to students who have been accepted to particular colleges and universities, you'll find that you begin to develop a sense of what type of student certain schools look for in an applicant. You'll see trends in the types of grades and coursework that make students good matches for certain schools and, for many, you'll no doubt discover that your grades and early test scores are a wonderful match. Along the way, you might also come across others where your academic record falls short of what the school wants to see. (Remember the rule, though: eighty percent of the schools *will* accept eighty percent of applicants - and that includes you!)

It's also important to remember that admission to any school never a guarantee – even for students whose academic records are flawless. The famous schools you read about every year – the ones who make the news with their precipitously low acceptance rates and therefore get everyone at school whispering - are a challenge for each and every student to gain admission to. Their admissions offices literally have their pick of the best of the best high school students in the United States and from around the world! This affords their admissions officers the luxury of being able to hand craft a freshman class that looks exactly the way they want it to. If the orchestra needs additional violas to fill open seats one year, the admissions officers can favor viola players come decision time. If the physics department has extra space for new physics majors and wants them to be female, the lucky girls who have indicated an interest in following that path when they submitted their applications will find their way to the top of the stack and will get an acceptance letter instead of one of their male counterparts. That's why a denial from an elite college should never be taken personally. (Likewise, an acceptance to one doesn't necessarily mean that the school is the right fit for you. It just means that you have something that they're looking for and your application was in the right place at the right time with the right features. You should absolutely be proud to get in, but don't forget that the ball is still in your court come decision time. Maybe the top school is your first choice, but maybe another school is where your heart lies.)

Sometimes the best strategy to adopt when you begin your formal college search is to simply utilize the resources you currently have close at hand. Use Naviance or your favorite web search engine and look up colleges that intrigue you to learn more. Schedule a meeting with your high school counselor to discuss these initial thoughts and findings and, while you're there, see if he or she can suggest potential schools to add to the mix. Perhaps you've also heard about a big university through their famous sports teams or you've read about the equestrian exploits of another interesting-sounding school in *The Chronicle of the Horse* and you want to learn more. Maybe you passed a friend in the school hallway wearing a sweatshirt with a university name scrawled across it or you want to know if your father's alma mater would be a good fit for you too. Colleges are all around you - but that doesn't mean you should sit down with a goal to come up with a list of thirty schools right off the bat. Instead, sit down with the intent to familiarize yourself with what's out there and what looks like it might be a potential match based on academic, equestrian, or extracurricular factors. (Just as in horse shopping, it takes time and effort to develop an eye for what appeals to you and what doesn't. Once you've seen fifty horses or so, you're better able to articulate why you liked certain ones better than others; you'll find that the same approach works just as well when it comes to comparing colleges.)

As you continue to develop your "eye for a college," read about the types of majors that are out there and the programs certain schools offer. Pull out a map and learn about the location where certain schools are found: Is it urban? Rural? Is the campus a part of the community or does it stand alone in the middle of nowhere? Certain characteristics will begin to stand out the more you look and you'll also find that more questions will develop for you along the way.

For example, if you read about a university with a program called leadership studies and you want to learn more about what such a program entails. Your first step would be to visit that school's web site and investigate the program - what are the classes like? What are the backgrounds of the professors teaching them? What careers do students move into after graduation? Then you could return to your search engine window and see which other schools might offer a similar program or major. You can then visit their web sites to make comparisons and see what appeals to you there. It's really no different than finding a particular sire that you like for his ability to produce top equitation horses and doing a search for other horses that fall within the same bloodline – and just as with horses, you'll no doubt begin to see patterns and trends emerge. It's only after you've begun to develop a somewhat educated eye that you should begin to truly *list* schools for consideration as the time to apply approaches – and don't worry if it seems too long at first. You can always cut it down later.

As the initial list takes shape, take the opportunity to let the schools know of your interest in them. Even though the Internet makes being a stealthy college searcher easy by allowing you to obtain a lot of information about a college without revealing very much about yourself, it's become very important to college admissions officers that students take the time to demonstrate their interest in the schools to which they plan to apply. Such interest can sometimes even be the tipping point that determines whether or not a student is accepted! Schools want to enroll students who show through their actions that they want to be there, so make sure that you communicate with them.

Taking the initiative to contact the school also allows admissions officers to put you on their radar and show the interest that they have in you in return. They'll send packets of information in the mail and contact you over email. Some schools may also wish to send you updates via text message or will encourage you to follow them on Twitter or another social media platform. (If you allow them to view your social media feeds or your status is set to be publicly viewable, make sure that you keep your sites professional or tighten up all of your privacy settings before you contact the colleges! Smart social media use can go a long way toward making you an appealing candidate in the eyes of the admissions office – just as unwise social media use can sometimes be result in denial of your application.)

Don't fear that colleges will bombard you with useless information, either - much of the information colleges want to share with you will turn out to be very helpful and can help you learn to gauge the personalities of the different schools before you even set foot on their campus for your first visit. Getting the name and contact information for the specific admissions counselor for your high school or region can also help your two-way dialogue with the college go smoothly. You can locate this person by visiting the admissions office webpages, which often feature links to help you locate your counselor by high school or region.

What if you decide later that you won't apply to a particular school and you don't want to learn any more about them? You can easily remove yourself from their mailing list by sending a quick email to their general admissions account or calling the admissions office to request that you be removed. (You might think it seems rude to say "no" to a school, but the admissions staff won't be offended by your rejection; they would prefer to spend their time recruiting students who really want to be there and if you're not among that group, you will free up their time for the others.)

While it might not be your favorite form of communication, email is the usual method preferred by college faculty and staff – including the admissions office – when they want to share information with you. In fact, some schools will even send your admission decision, housing, and financial aid information to your email inbox as opposed to using more traditional (old-fashioned) methods like the U.S. Mail. If you don't currently have an email account - either personally or through your high school – the start of your college search is the time to create one. (Thanks to smart phones and tablets, you might already have a personal account; if you don't, your devices can make it easier to receive and manage your email.)

Many students who already have an email account prefer to keep their college communications separate from everything else in order to keep their busy lives organized. If you choose to do so and plan to create a specific college email account for yourself, be sure to select a professional-sounding address, such as Sarah.Smith01@collegemail.com or even just SarahCollege@collegemail.com. It's strongly recommended not to make any overly political or religious statements in your email title, though you would be fine with something that shares a little of your personality, like SarahDressage@collegemail.com. Also be careful to avoid anything that is an inside joke with your friends or downright silly, such as BriansXGirlfriend@collegemail.com or DontBeThatGuy@collegemail.com. Then, be sure to remind yourself to *check* your email on a regular basis so you don't miss anything!

Social media users (Facebook, Twitter, Instagram, Tumblr, etc.) should also be aware that college and university admissions offices are examining students' social media profiles during the admission process more frequently these days. Make sure that all of your privacy settings are set to be as secure as possible, choose profile pictures that are appropriate and flattering, and don't post anything questionable online - *ever*.

A quick Google search of your own name can help you evaluate your online footprint; if anything alarming is out there, you must be prepared to address it with your prospective colleges. In 2013, the Kaplan Test Preparation staff learned that thirty one percent of colleges use social media checkups to determine whether or not to admit students – a number that was up from 2012. (Of course, the best advice of all is always to never post anything online that you don't want made public.)

Equestrians should also do a Google (or other similar search engine) check for their name and the word "horse" or else the word "equestrian." If you've ever competed, there is the possibility that your horse show results, photos, and even video footage of you exist on the Internet that you are unaware of but that a potential college coach might find if your name comes up on his or her list of interested recruits. If the video in question features your ride at the North American Junior and Young Rider Championships last year and you're proud of it, then you have nothing to worry about. Conversely, if your friend posted the video she took on the day that you both decided to jump your horses over a series of hay bales while seated backwards and you weren't wearing helmets, you might drop to the bottom of the coach's prospects list very quickly.

Finally, it's important that you use *primary* sources to obtain your college information so that you can ensure that the data you're working with is as accurate as possible. Primary sources are original documents or pieces of information that come directly from the object (or, in this case, the college) itself. Primary source information hasn't been interpreted or evaluated through another channel before it reaches you, so examples of primary sources for colleges and universities include the school's own web sites, parts of your school's Naviance site, and your own personal experiences during a visit to campus. One evening during the fall or spring, your high school or a local community college might also hold a college fair and bring in the representatives from hundreds of colleges and universities one evening to serve as primary source information.

(**Author's Note**: This can also be a great way to get your name on a lot of the mailing lists of the schools that you're interested in. Take some peel and stick address labels with you and the process will be quick and easy!)

Secondary sources are those which have been subjected to someone else's interpretation or evaluation – web sites with forums like *College Confidential, College Prowler, Cappex*, and *RateMyProfessors.com*. Though many admission and counseling professionals participate on the sites and most information is entirely factual, the forums allow any interested users to post their personal opinions about the schools in question and – while those opinions may have merit for you in the end – it's better for you to reach your own conclusions than to assume that someone else's research directly applies to you. (Remember - the most valuable opinion when it comes to choosing the right school for you is always going to be *your own*.)

While there really is no "best" time to begin making your college list, you should begin thinking generally about college as early as your sophomore year of high school. In your junior year, the list should begin to take real shape (even though juniors normally sit for the ACT and/or SAT and preparation for the tests can often be very time-consuming). If your search is well underway by that time, it helps to reduce stress during testing season because you'll have one less thing to worry about. By August 1 of your senior year, your list should be finalized and you should be poised and ready to begin the process of filling out your college applications. The bottom line is that high school moves quickly, so if you think the list will be a major undertaking for you (and chances are, it will), the sooner you can begin thinking about and examining your college options, the better it will be in the end.

Also remember as you search that choosing schools to put on your list of choices isn't actually choosing a *school* itself – instead, you're choosing options to examine more closely. Just as in the previously used example of horse shopping, no horse that you try is ever completely perfect, but you find that you always get along better with some than with others. Colleges are the same – each one has its own quirks and blemishes, but there is one out there that will be right for you. As you get to know your potential schools through research and campus visits, you'll begin to see things that you really like about them and other things that you don't necessarily care for. If a school is the right fit for you, though, all of the positives will be things that you love and all of the negatives will be things that you can comfortably live with. It's exactly like the moment you find the horse you want to buy and you think he's perfect in every way - except that you wanted bay and he's gray. The horse isn't perfect, but he's *right*. Your college will be exactly the same – not perfect, just *right*.

6
THE CAMPUS VISIT – WHEN, WHY, AND HOW?

"Campus visits are a whirlwind. Also, everyone on a campus visit day (if you go on an organized event) is there to make the school look and sound its very best. You won't find out the little negative details until you show up and have been at the school for a while [and discover] the dorms look nothing like the tour room and everything is "highlighted" for visits."
Lauren, IHSA hunt seat alumna

By the time you complete the initial list of colleges that are of interest to you, you'll undoubtedly have been bombarded with countless images of beautiful, sunny campuses from a variety of web sites and glossy brochures. Images of college life are all fairly similar no matter what school you're looking at: The students are happily attired in sweatshirts bearing the school's name or mascot and they stroll down sidewalks strewn with fallen leaves on a golden autumn day, textbooks in hand as they share a laugh.

It looks perfect, doesn't it? It's everything that popular culture has led you to believe that college should be.

Though these iconic images have come to exemplify college life in the United States for every high school student who's ever picked up a brochure, unfortunately they don't do much to help you differentiate between schools. The residence hall photo from Campus A looks just like the residence hall photo from Campus B, except that Campus A's colors are blue and gold and Campus B is decked out in red and white.

Think the equestrian program brochures can help you tell them apart? Think again:

Upon observation, you'll discover that nearly every hunt seat program web site and brochure prominently features a beautiful hunter (usually bay or chestnut) jumping a natural fence (brush or coop), its knees up and perfectly square and its rider attired so flawlessly that not even George Morris could criticize. Western programs likewise have two favored variations – either a glamorous rail shot of a rider with a perfect seat and a flat back aboard a horse whose head set is immaculate *or* an exciting action shot taken at the moment a reining horse hits the peak of his slide with dirt flying up on either side and his mane blowing back in dramatic fashion.

Summary: Each image you see for a college or university or for any one of its programs (including equestrian teams) is carefully chosen before it's published. It's marketing at its very best - and very confusing if you're examining the schools from afar.

As a prospective college student, there's really only one way to discover which crowd of happily strolling students – or which barn of perfectly turned out riders – you will want to join: You must the campuses for yourself. Even in our current age of live streaming video and social media, there is absolutely no college search tool in existence that is more valuable or more influential than an in-person campus visit.

That's right, only by actually setting foot on campus and having face to face conversations with staff, faculty, and current students will you know if a particular school feels comfortable to you. You must discover firsthand the culture of the school – what type of people are there, what the atmosphere on campus is on a typical weekday – so you will know if a particular campus is the place you can see yourself after high school.

Before you schedule your trip, however, realize that a campus visit done correctly is not merely a casual stroll across the quadrangle, a quick peak inside the dining hall, and a stop in the bookstore to purchase a t-shirt before you leave. Instead, it's a half (or sometimes even a full) day commitment of time and energy on your part. You'll need to take advantage of every opportunity available to you and learn what strengths a particular campus has.

In order to facilitate this kind of deep exploration, you should engage in the following activities on a campus visit:

- A guided campus tour
- An information session and/or informational interview with an admissions staff member.
  (**Author's Note:** An informational interview is different from an evaluative interview; notably, an informational interview is not strictly for the purposes of determining admission status, but instead allows the student to familiarize him or herself with certain aspects of the school and the admissions process that he or she finds unclear.)
- Lunch (or any meal) in a campus dining hall
- Sit in on one or two classes in your area of interest
- Meet with a faculty member in your area of interest
- Meet with the riding coach (or with members of the campus equestrian club if the coach runs his or her own facility off-campus)
- Observe riding lessons or the equestrian team's practice
- Grab coffee or a snack at the favorite campus hang out and chat casually with students there
- Drive (or walk) through the surrounding town/community

If you have limited time available during your first visit to a campus, going on tour and attending a campus information session can be enough to tell you whether or not you'd like to return again on a later date to learn more. (Those two items can usually be accomplished within a three or four hour period.) Second – and even third – visits to campus can be spent observing classes, eating in the dining hall, and getting more in-depth information on particular programs that interest you.

Arranging a campus visit can be as easy as going to the college or university's web site to find out what opportunities they have available. The admissions page for undergraduate students (sometimes listed as "First Time Freshman") will normally have a calendar that displays the dates that the office is open for tours and the times that are available on those days. The visit page might also list the dates for campus open house or visitation programs, which run for a full day and are designed to focus solely on a particular program to give students with specific interests a chance to investigate them in-depth.

As you formulate a schedule of campus visits, you might find that you come across two other specific types of visits that are offered by some colleges and are a little more structured than a normal weekday visit or campus open house: the **official visit** and the **overnight visit.**

In simple terms, an **official visit** is an athletic recruiting visit that is paid for in part or in whole by the university instead of the student's family. The goal of an **official visit** is to bring a heavily-recruited student athlete to campus so that the coaching staff can learn more about the athlete and demonstrate to him or her why they believe the school will be a good fit for that athlete's abilities. It can be a fairly big deal to be invited on an **official visit** because it speaks to how highly a particular program thinks of the recruit and how focused they are on getting that student to enroll in their school in the fall.

Because of their NCAA status, NCEA equestrian programs are allowed to offer **official visits** to recruits whom they might be considering for an athletic scholarship or for any rider who is simply a top prospect for the program. If you are one of these lucky students, it's important to know that the regulations of the NCAA and NCEA limit recruits to no more than five **official visits** in total during their entire high school career and no more than one **official visit** to any particular school. For students with more than five schools demonstrating strong interest in inviting them for a visit, some decisions need to be made before the offers can be accepted.

Because **official visits** are scheduled at the behest of coaches, they are typically arranged through the athletic department as opposed to being organized by someone in the admissions office (though this can vary by institution). Because of budget structures and team resources, it's also important to know that not all schools or college equestrian teams offer **official visits** to their recruits – so while it's an honor to be asked to come on one, it isn't the only way prospective student athletes can get to campus.

For example, you're always more than welcome to attend an **unofficial visit**, which is any trip to a campus that is paid for entirely by the student and his or her family. Any of the individual or open house visits mentioned at the beginning of this chapter are **unofficial visits** and provide a lot of really good opportunities for you to acquaint yourself with a particular school. What's more, per NCAA/NCEA regulations, students may visit a particular campus as many times as they would like to in an **unofficial** capacity. They may also meet with the equestrian coach on these visits as many times as the coach's schedule will permit. There really aren't too many restrictions that are placed on an **unofficial visit** (though all prospective athletes should avoid taking any gifts that are offered to them by coaches or admissions staff members unless those gifts are offered to all students, athlete and non-athlete alike).

Because they are self-funded, **unofficial visits** can be arranged by you and your family through the school admissions office – though depending on the institution, the athletic department can help you to arrange the schedule for these visits as well if you're already in contact with the coach. The main thing to remember is to use one point of contact on campus when arranging all of the elements of your trip so that you avoid a conflicted schedule and are able to see and do everything that you want to.

Overnight visits are exactly what the name implies – an opportunity for prospective students to get a "behind-the-scenes" look at a particular school by spending the night on campus in a residence hall with current students. Depending on the school and its internal policies, this type of visit can either be offered by the admissions office or by the athletic department – or the two might work in tandem on the arrangements. No matter who sets it up, however, when planning an overnight visit, the staff try to pair prospective students with current students who share the same interests (for example, putting an English major who rides on the western IHSA team with a prospect who hopes to do the same).

The goal for everyone is to give the visitor real insight into what her life might be like if she enrolls. There are even some schools that put together full overnight programs that bring a large group of prospective students in to spend the night with a particular team or club on the same date, with different social events scheduled to entertain the guests.

Not all campuses offer or allow **overnight visits** for prospective students, however, because of the liability involved with bringing sixteen and seventeen-year-old high school students onto a campus with eighteen to twenty-two year-olds; notably, some activities are legal for the older students but illegal for the younger ones and it can be risky to mix the groups. Even if you forego a formally-scheduled overnight program in favor of just paying a visit to a trusted older friend from home who attends a college you're interested in, it's important that you and your family discuss whether or not this is a good option for you before you arrive on campus so that you can be prepared to address any uncomfortable situations that may come up.

Despite the potential risks involved, **overnight visits** shouldn't be viewed in an entirely negative context, however – they hold a valuable place in terms of your options for getting the most complete picture of a school that you can. What's more, they can be extremely valuable in helping you choose between two schools that are very similar on paper and continue to seem alike after your daytime campus visits. You might even meet a particular group of people on a campus overnight with whom you instantly click and you'll select that campus to be your college home as a result. Yet you must be prepared in case certain uncomfortable or even dangerous situations occur and it's important that you and your parents take this possibility into account when deciding whether or not an **overnight visit** is the right choice for you. Having a frank and honest talk about it before you schedule your stay can help all of you feel better-prepared for every eventuality.

On a regular (unofficial) campus visit, you'll find that the two most common activities offered are a campus tour and an information session led by a member of the admissions staff. In fact, most schools offer two or three tour and information session pairings during a regular week day to accommodate as many visitors as possible. You can use your estimated travel time and the types of other activities that you would like to engage in while on campus as an indication of which session to choose when you're scheduling your trip.

(**Author's Note:** It's best if you arrive in time for the very first tour and information session of the day so that you have the most options available to you afterwards; if, however, you're going to pair the visit with an overnight stay either in the area or on campus, perhaps a better choice is to do the very last tour and information session and do your other activities on campus the following day.)

As a general rule, the tours are led by current students who are employed by the admissions office as tour guides, student ambassadors, or whatever other term that particular campus has for them. The tours themselves can be as small as one-on-one (just your family and the guide) or as a large as fifty people and one guide. The majority of tours are walking tours, but some larger campuses may utilize a bus or golf cart shuttle system so that tour groups can see more of campus in a shorter period of time. It's ideal if you can be part of a smaller tour group, as less of a crowd gives you and your parents the opportunity to ask more questions that are specific to you, as well as allowing the guide the flexibility to customize the tour stops to your interests. Yet larger tours tend to be the norm, so if you find yourself in a big group, position yourself as close to the guide as possible so that you can hear properly. Also, don't hesitate to speak up anytime you have a question – even if you have to raise your hand and be called on like you do in school. Guides who are accustomed to giving large tours will utilize several stopping points on the tour so that they can corral the group and share information in a way that allows everyone to hear what they're saying; however, since these stopping points are often far apart, you can use the walking time to ask specific questions of the guide if you're near the front.

Parents often have questions for tour guides as well and are certainly encouraged to ask them – just as long as all of the students' questions have been addressed *first*! Too often on tours, well-meaning parents monopolize the conversation between themselves and the guides and leave the prospective students to listen in silence. It's not always intentional, of course, and most parents will even agree that it's better if the students can be in charge of the flow of the tour conversation. (After all, they're the ones who might eventually attend the school!) So in order not to talk *too* much on a campus tour, parents should monitor themselves carefully. It's okay to help begin a flow of questions if the students in the group are hesitant to begin, but once you get the first ones to engage, it's best to fall silent and listen carefully as the students all interact with one another. (Who knows – you might even learn *more* that way!)

It's also important to note that, while the student guide leading you across campus is employed by the college's admissions office, he or she is by no means an admissions *counselor*. Tour guides are selected and hired based on their outgoing personalities and ability to convey information about the experiential side of campus. From their knowledge of classes and professors, to their knowledge of athletics and student life, tour guides are experts in everything you could possibly want to know.

They are *not*, however, well-versed or trained in the areas of financial aid, admission statistics, or the school's business operations. If you have questions about tuition costs, scholarship possibilities, or the specifics of the school's financial aid awarding policies, you'll have to hold them until after the tour. (It's also a huge no-no – and rude! - to ask the student about his or her own individual financial aid package.)

In a nutshell, the tour is your opportunity to inquire about student life on a particular campus. Great questions to ask include:

What kinds of clubs are offered?

How easy is it to be involved in student government?

What's going on around here tonight after classes finish?

How are students informed about social events – email? Social media?

What's the most fun thing to do here?

Do you like the food?

What was your favorite/least favorite thing about living in the dorms?

Do upperclassman have to live off-campus or are dorms an option all four years?

You might also inquire about the guide's favorite classroom experience(s), what a typical weekend is like on campus, and why he or she chose to attend the institution when it came time to make the final decision.

After you've been on a handful of tours, you'll also gain an idea of how much both the campus tours and the guides can begin to resemble one another. These similarities exist quite simply because the majority of campus tours are scripted in such totality that even the answers you receive to your questions may begin to sound the same! Sometimes, the stories that are told aren't even the guide's own personal experiences, but are instead a broad generalization that refers to the experiences of some students on campus (but not all). It comes down to simple economics, unfortunately – colleges need students to fill their classrooms and tour guides need jobs. Those who deviate from the script can be cut from the program and, with tour guide positions often among the most coveted and highest-paying on campus, it's rare for guides to do or say anything that could jeopardize their employment.

Before you throw your hands up in frustration at this revelation, however, take a moment to understand that tour guides or admissions offices are in the business of lying to families or engaging in full-scale cover ups regarding certain facets of their campus facilities or the student body. Instead, be aware that the tour guide is just one person on campus and therefore is just one source of information relevant to your college search. In fact, the majority you will encounter *are* completely truthful and are comfortable speaking off-script with families. (Still, by the time you've been on two or three tours, you'll have developed a fairly reliable sense of whether a tour is genuine or whether you'd like to wander campus a bit on your own afterwards to chat with "regular" students to get their candid opinions.)

After your tour, you can direct the harder-hitting questions – money, admission rates, etc. – to the admissions staff during an information session or during a one-on-one informational interview. (Don't panic at the word "interview," though! As noted previously, an **informational interview** is different from an admission interview because, in an informational interview, the purpose of the meeting is for you to ask questions about the college and its programs and for the admissions representative to answer and to get to know a little bit more about you as a person. While the information you share will most likely end up in your application file, the questions they ask won't be as direct as those that would be asked in an evaluative admission interview, which would more strongly influence the final decision as to whether or not you are accepted.)

The majority of admission office information sessions feature a multimedia presentation of some kind, so be sure to have something on hand to take notes with to help you remember everything later. (You may even wish to jot some questions down before you get to campus if you know that there is a specific program you want to know more about or if you saw something on the web site or in a brochure that brought up a question for you.) Some information sessions may also feature a student panel so that you can hear about the experiences of more students than just your tour guide.

When preparing for your campus visit and thinking up questions to ask on tour, it's advisable that you not ask very simple questions that can be answered easily by surfing the school's web site. Examples of these questions include: How many students attend the school? What is tuition this year? Do you have a biology major? What kinds of clubs and organizations are on campus?

The reason for you to prepare so fully is twofold: First, it shows that you have done some homework and researched the school before your arrival on campus. (Doing so demonstrates your interest and shows you to be a conscientious and organized individual.) Second, it maximizes the time that you spend on campus so that you can get more in-depth and valuable information from current students, faculty, and staff members rather than just asking them to rattle off statistics.

If you're able to sit in and observe a class in session during your visit, be sure to seize the chance! It will provide you with more valuable information and immerse you in the academic life of the college. The key thing to remember in this instance is that your purpose for being in class is to gain a sense of what the professor's teaching style is, how the students take in information, and what you feel like when you're there. Ask yourself the following:

- Does the professor lecture to a large group or is there a roundtable discussion?
- Are there handouts or a PowerPoint presentation?
- Are students taking notes with pen and paper or on laptops? (If they're using laptops, are they engaged in the class or checking their Twitter feed?)
- Is the class discussion lively or passive?
- Does this look like the classroom experience you imagined? Does it appeal to you or not?
- Do you think you could learn in this type of environment?

Don't focus too specifically on what is being taught if it seems overwhelming at first – remember, the students in the class have studied the topic for a lot longer than you have! Sometimes the professor may even call on you and ask for your opinion regarding the discussion and it's okay to say that you don't know yet because you don't know the topic well enough. If you're feeling brave, however, don't hesitate to offer an answer!

After the class (or before it begins, if time permits), take the opportunity to meet the students sitting near you and chat with the professor if he or she is willing. Just as you wouldn't buy a horse without a thorough veterinary exam to show exactly what's going on with its bones, ligaments, and other vital systems, you wouldn't necessarily want to purchase an education without vetting it first either. A classroom visit is a great way to vet the academic programs at the school and, in particular, the major that you're most interested in. The professor could one day be *your* professor and the students seated near you could one day be *your* classmates – find out if they're the type of people you can see yourself learning from (and with)!

As an equestrian and a prospective team member, it's also important for you and your parents to check out the equestrian facilities where the team practices and competes, as well as to meet the people involved. If the school oversees the riding program and owns the facility, it should be easy to schedule a visit to the barn during or after your visit to campus. The admissions office can help set it up for you in most cases, though sometimes times you'll need to contact the equestrian coach or an office or stable manager directly. If, however, the equestrian team is a student-governed club, you may need to reach out to the student leaders on your own (though the admission staff might be able to assist by giving you names and email addresses) or contact the off-site coach directly via email or phone. Often, the barn is a short drive away from campus so you'll want to wrap up your scheduled commitments there before you head out.

When you schedule the equestrian portion of your campus visit, the most important thing to remember is the following:

Whether the barn is school-owned or a private facility, *always* make an appointment with the coach or another equestrian program representative. Horse people are notoriously busy and because the unexpected can happen at a barn on any given day, there's no guarantee that it won't happen during your visit. Farriers and vets are in and out all day, lessons come and go, and horses are turned out, brought in, and inevitably find ways to get loose or into trouble at any given moment. If you schedule an appointment for a particular time, you get an official spot on the busy calendar and it will be your best chance to get face time with the coach or a program representative. There's always the small chance that an emergency might occur and pull them away, but most coaches will make time for recruits when they know you're coming – or at the very least make sure that a student or another staff member is available to answer your questions and show you around. If you show up unexpectedly or at the wrong time, there's no guarantee that anyone will be available to meet with you and you might feel brushed aside. The best way to avoid that situation is to be courteous and organized by making arrangements in advance and allowing the program staff the opportunity to be courteous and welcoming to you in return.

Some equestrian team coaches might invite you to ride while you're visiting (as a sort of "pre-tryout"), while others will allow you to observe their lessons but will not allow you to climb into the saddle. If you ride while you're on campus, you may be required to pay a lesson fee as well as sign liability paperwork (or have your parents sign it if you aren't yet eighteen). You'll need to inquire with the specific program when you arrange your visit. You'll also need to inquire about what gear you should bring with you and what will be provided by the program (spurs, jumping bats, etc.).

As thrilling as the offer of a riding lesson from a college coach sounds, however, it isn't always your best choice in terms of being able to evaluate the program. In fact, if the ride that's being offered is part of a regular lesson within a group of team riders or even just a private lesson with one of the instructors, you might benefit more by observing the lesson than you will by riding in it. There are two reasons for this:

Reason One: If you're not riding, you're free to direct your full attention to what the instructor tells his or her students and to watch how each one responds. **Observe the teaching style of the lesson:**

Does the coach ask questions or just give commands?

Is the lesson rapid-fire or are there a series of breaks?

Does everyone ride the same horse the whole time or do they switch?

Is there a time for questions and answers at the end?

Observe the horses in the lesson:

Are they in good weight?

What about their equipment – boots or wraps for jumping, clean saddle pads, etc.?

Are they generally schoolmasters or do they look squirrely?

Finally, pay close attention to the riders' behavior:

What attire is required?

Do they all ride in relatively the same style or is everyone unique?

Do they look confident or confused?

Most importantly, do they seem to be having fun?

Conversely, if you're riding in the lesson, your focus will be split between the lesson and the horse you're on and you will have to worry more about steering and riding – especially if you aren't accustomed to riding in group lessons in the first place. Because less of your attention will be available to really get a feel for what the coach's expectations are for his or her team riders, you might not find that it's as valuable of an exercise as you had hoped it would be.

Reason Two: Riding in a strange environment on a strange horse will most likely make you nervous and self-conscious. Of course, there's nothing really *wrong* with a few nerves – participating in horse shows might have the same effect on you - but the primary purpose of your visit to the equestrian center is to learn about the riding team, coaches, facilities, and lesson options available to students and decide if they will work for you. Every program at every barn has its own culture whether it's a college team's home facility or a regular lesson barn in your home town, so the most important thing you can do during your college search is determine which environment will be your best fit.

When it comes to the question of whether or not to take a trial ride, he last thing you want to do is have a bad lesson at the end of a great campus visit - something like that could knock a school off your list for no good reason other than you got nervous in front of the coach and made some silly errors that haunted you after. Or perhaps your particular lesson paired you with a horse with whom you discovered a horrible personality conflict and it turned you off the program and the school as a result. Little things like that are really inconsequential and, in most cases you'd just brush them aside, but in the college search process, they tend to get blown up to epic proportions. Thus, if you take every opportunity to control the situation and avoid putting such high pressure on yourself, you'll feel a lot less stress and find that you're more easily able to pinpoint the strengths and weaknesses of different college riding opportunities without getting overly emotional about what happened in a lesson or which program had the horse that made you miserable.

A few final notes about campus visits before you consult your calendar and sign up:

Campus visits aren't necessarily a one-time thing. Campus visits are an ongoing part of junior and senior year and, while it isn't necessary that you visit every campus before you apply as a senior, it can be extremely helpful to do so. If you are accepted to a school that you haven't yet visited, make sure you make the trip to see it in person long before your final decision will be required – and if you're accepted to several schools that you really enjoyed visiting earlier, make appointments to go back and see different things so that you can get a more complete picture of what your life might be like as a student there.

Avoid Saturday (and/or Sunday) visits whenever possible. A Saturday or Sunday on *any* college or university campus is the absolute worst day to learn anything valuable about the school. Sure you may find that a lot of schools offer weekend visit options to accommodate people's busy schedules, but if you *really* want to see what authentic, everyday life on campus is like, a far better choice is to see it on a weekday.

What happens on weekends on a college campus? The answer is normally one of two things: you'll either discover the crazy atmosphere of a big sporting or social event (lots of people, limited or restricted parking, and a party-like atmosphere that may or may not be indicative of the normal campus personality) or the ghost town-like stupor of a weekend with no special activities or home athletics where students spend the day sleeping late and catching up on laundry and homework. Many campuses even serve breakfast foods in the dining halls until well into the afternoon to account for the adjusted sleep schedule of a slow Saturday!

What's more, faculty members are very rarely available to meet on weekends and coaches are usually out traveling with their teams, so it's very hard to find a time to speak with the people you most need to direct your questions to. And if you can't get your questions answered, then are you really getting any value in the trip? (Campus visits – especially those to schools located a distance from your home town – aren't always inexpensive and you'll want to get the most return on your investment of both time and money when you schedule them.)

Finally, what you see on campus on one weekend isn't necessarily what you would see if you arrived on an entirely different weekend. So skip the Saturday visit whenever possible.

Never leave campus without contact information for people whom you've met or who will work directly with you. The most important contact information to have is that of the admissions staff member who is specifically assigned to work with you (whether you meet them in person or not). Most are assigned either by state and/or region or by specific high school. Your assigned admissions counselor is your point of contact on campus and the one who will most likely read and review your application file. In addition to the admission counselor or representative, you might also want contact information for a professor in your area of interest (or his or her graduate teaching assistant) so you can ask academic questions when they come up. Finally, you will also want the contact information for the equestrian team coach or (in the case of a student-run club team) the team captain or club president – whoever will be the best person for you to direct questions to during your search. (And if you're an underclass student in tenth or eleventh grade, remember that student contacts generally chance from year to year, so you might need updated information by the time your senior year rolls around.)

Dress appropriately for the tour – and the weather!
Appropriate tour attire is always casual and clean; if you couldn't get it past your high school's dress code or the eye of a strict grandparent, don't wear it on a tour. Likewise, don't overdress for the occasion either – as previously stated, most campus tours are *walking* tours so you'll need to wear comfortable, practical shoes. What's more, individual expressions of style are fine when it comes to clothing and accessories, but it's best to avoid wearing pieces of clothing that reference controversial issues or advertise rival schools. For touring the equestrian facilities, always remember your barn-appropriate footwear as well.

Finally, don't forget to take the weather forecast into account when you pack. Umbrellas might be provided on loan by the admissions office if the sky suddenly opens up, but you might also need to provide your own. Depending on the time of year and the school's location, jackets, hats, gloves, or sunglasses might also be necessary for your comfort. Travel prepared!

Silence and ignore your phone. It's great that you instantly want to share with all of your friends the wonderful time that you're having on your tour, but be sure to save your social networking for *after* the tour and the other scheduled visit activities. Using the camera on your phone is permitted (as long as you don't use it so much that you distract everyone else in the group) and it can be useful in helping you record something memorable for later. Texting, talking, or other similar activities, however, are not only rude to the tour guide and distracting to the other families in the group, but it also diverts your full attention from learning about a school you've traveled a long way to see.

(Parents, even though campus tours might fall into the middle of your office's busy season, you're going to have to follow the same silent phone rules as your children – and you should set a good example for them. If you need to make or take an important call, please separate yourself from the group in order to be courteous to everyone else and re-join them later.)

Have fun! The college market is one that is geared far more in favor of the buyer (you) than the seller (the school), so chances are you'll find the red carpet rolled out to welcome you when you set foot on campus. Even so, you don't have to fall in love with every campus you see and the whole point of the experience should be to enlighten you as to whether or not a particular school will be a great home for you for four years. Will it offer you the sort of support and guidance you'll need to be successful in the future or should you look elsewhere? If the visit experience isn't fun, then chances are you won't have fun as an enrolled student at that school either. But if you really enjoy yourself and meet some wonderful people, you might be well on your way to making your choice!

7

I WANT TO BE AN OFFICIALLY RECRUITED ATHLETE – HOW DO I ACHIEVE MY GOAL?

"Team life is hard; you're going to be riding horses that test you, you're going to draw horses that are tough to ride, and you're going to ride horses that make you have those "Aaaaaaaaaah, this is the life!" moments. But probably more rough draws than good draws and it's going to be hard to take that in stride sometimes."
Kate, IHSA western alumna

Perhaps over the course of the previous six chapters, you've decided that your ultimate goal as a college equestrian will be to ride at the varsity level through the National Collegiate Equestrian Association (NCEA). Or perhaps riding with the NCEA has been your goal for some time and you picked up this book for specific information to guide you through the NCEA recruitment and eligibility process. Either way, becoming an officially recruited athlete through the NCEA is a very specific, regimented, and detailed process that requires a lot of organization and scheduling on your part. If you want to successfully navigate the transition from your high school equestrian activities to the college level, everything – from your primary riding discipline to the type and amount of competitions you enter, the grades and test scores you achieve, and the high school classes you take each semester – must be correctly documented and reported to the NCAA as well as to your prospective universities. To help you better understand what you'll need to do, this chapter will walk you through the steps required and outline some of the considerations you should keep in mind as you move forward.

Before you read any farther, however, remember the description of the NCEA that was given in Chapter Two.

Specifically, recall that only female equestrians are allowed to compete in the NCEA, which is an officially recognized emerging sport through the National Collegiate Athletic Association (NCAA). In order to become a fully sponsored NCAA sport, there need to be forty Division I and II schools participating in equestrian in the U.S.; currently there are twenty-two universities in the United States that host women's varsity equestrian on their athletic rosters – eighteen in NCAA Division I and four in NCAA Division II.

As a prospective NCEA rider, your first step is to become **eligible** to be recruited and compete under their umbrella. Eligibility for equestrian athletes and all prospective NCAA athletes is determined primarily by the courses that you take during your four years of high school and your performance in them.

What does that mean specifically?

In the case of prospective NCAA/NCEA athletes, it means that they must not only work hard to achieve top grades, but must also complete sixteen required "core" courses by the time they graduate from high school. (The NCAA defines a core course as those that fall within the divisions of English, math, social studies, natural/physical sciences, and foreign language and/or philosophy/religion.)

By the time the athlete reaches the seventh semester of her high school career (which is traditionally the first semester of her senior year), she must have completed ten of the required core courses and is not allowed to re-take any of the ten in an effort to improve her cumulative grade point average. This is because the NCAA/NCEA requires **eligible** athletes to graduate with a cumulative GPA that is *above* 2.3 (for Division I eligibility) and *above* 2.0 (for Division II eligibility).

(**Author's Note:** The NCAA recently altered their eligibility course requirements for all students who will graduate during or after the year 2016. Though the change was minor and simply raised the minimum GPA that will be required to be considered **eligible**, it also allowed for recognition of different core courses in accordance with the U.S. government's "Common Core" standards. Changes like this to NCAA **eligibility** standards are not altogether uncommon as the face of primary and higher education continue to shift and change over time – which is why it's important for parents and students to educate themselves about the current standards that will apply to the student's class year.)

All prospective NCEA athletes are also required to take the SAT **or** the ACT to be considered eligible. (They may take both if they choose, but both tests are accepted equally by the organization so students are free to choose which one they prefer.) For Division I, a sliding scale that compares a student's GPA with her best single test score (from one administration) is used to determine eligibility. For Division II, a minimum SAT score of 820 (critical reading and math sections only) or a minimum ACT of 68 (the *sum* – not the *average* – of the English, math, reading, and science sections) is required. The student is responsible for having all of her scores sent directly to the NCAA from each test sitting.

(**Author's Note:** If a student takes the ACT one, two, or even three times, she must designate that a copy of each of her test results be sent to the NCAA at the time the test is taken; the NCAA will not accept test results in any other manner and will not recognize the validity of any test scores that may appear on a high school transcript.)

Ideally, because of the four-year curriculum requirements to become an eligible NCAA/NCEA college athlete, students and their parents should begin to plan for this path as early as ninth grade. For students, this ensures that you are able to take the correct courses over your four years and document your academic record correctly. If you're already in high school and just making the decision to become eligible, however, you don't need to worry. For the most part, the NCAA's core requirements mimic the graduation requirements set by each state for high school curriculum, so you should have no trouble becoming eligible at this stage – just keep in mind you might have some backtracking to do in order to make sure you haven't missed anything from earlier in your high school career.

As a high school junior, you must register with the NCAA's Eligibility Center (formerly known as the NCAA Clearinghouse) because doing so indicates your formal intent to become a recruited equestrian athlete. (Just as you demonstrate interest to colleges and universities, the NCAA wants you to formally declare your interest in athletics as well.) Once you've registered for the Eligibility Center, you'll have a profile online and a ten-digit identification number that coaches can later use to access your information and learn more about you.

High school juniors also have a little added paperwork to complete at the end of the school year, as you must request that your high school guidance office send a copy of your updated (official) high school transcript to the NCAA so that it can be added to your eligibility profile. (The transcript is what certifies that, to date, you have taken the correct core courses to achieve and maintain your eligibility.)

Are you bewildered yet - or afraid that you'll drown in paperwork before all is said and done?

You aren't alone!

To minimize confusion, the NCAA publishes an annual *Guide for the College-Bound Student Athlete* that provides step-by-step assistance and instruction for students who are going through the registration process and want to play NCAA varsity athletics. They also make sure to update it every school year. In fact, your guidance counselor might already have a copy on file for you to look at, as a lot of coaches and counselors use this tool to help them advise their students and to prevent oversight when it comes to documenting a student's academic record. If you're serious about becoming an officially recruited athlete, it's important for you to access the guide online (through the NCAA web site or at the Eligibility Center) and get your own copy, though. Download a PDF so that you can refer back frequently for the information you'll need over the course of your junior and senior years.

Beyond grades and test scores, it's particularly important as a prospective NCEA equestrian athlete that you develop and maintain a thorough record of your horse shows as well. This includes all horse show names and locations, the distance you traveled to get there and back (mileage), the amount of prize money you earned, and the expenses you incurred. (If you've competed in a lot of rated shows, the United States Equestrian Federation (USEF) online database and your local horse show organizations and clubs that keep track of year-end standings can be immensely helpful in this regard by posting the information in one place for you to access.)

Without this information – or worse, with inaccurate information – you can't be officially certified as an amateur athlete with the NCEA and can't be recruited. So if you have even the slightest inclination to become an NCEA equestrian after high school, track the information carefully so that you don't have to look it all up in a hurry as senior year approaches.

Don't panic at the use of the term **amateur** either.

Unlike at traditional equestrian competitions where amateurs and professionals are divided by carefully-outlined rules that are outlined by various equestrian governing bodies (USEF, USDF, AQHA, NRHA, etc.), intercollegiate equestrians who compete under the umbrella of the NCAA/NCEA are considered to be an **amateur** so long as their prize money earnings do not exceed the amount of expenses paid for competitions attended within the calendar year.

(Now do you understand why thorough accounting and saving the receipts for all expenses – is so important during your ninth through twelfth grade years?)

Also, if you join the NCEA team at your chosen school and then wish to ride and show with your home barn during the summer months, you must continue to keep complete and thorough financial records in order to retain your **amateur** athlete certification. (NCAA and NCEA student athletes must renew their amateur status for each of their four years of competitive eligibility.)

Once you've worked through the necessary steps to make yourself eligible to be recruited as an equestrian athlete, it's time to begin your school search for universities with NCEA teams and the right academic programs for your interests. As you investigate your options, you'll start to see trends emerge as you compare the various riding programs to one another. For example, the NCEA rules allow each team to have one head coach and two assistant coaches on staff. For most equestrian teams, it's rare to find a team that doesn't have at least two coaches. Depending on the academic offerings at the university, these coaches aren't always simply full-time riding instructors; instead, they are often full-time members of the university's athletic staff or part of the equine or animal science faculty who teach classes or oversee the daily operations of the equine facilities in addition to coaching and traveling with the equestrian teams.

When you're ready to reach out and make your first contact with these coaches, you'll need to know a few of the general guidelines for doing so. Namely: The NCAA does not regulate when you as a prospective student athlete may contact a coach, but they *do* regulate when and how a coach is able to respond to you. What this means is that a recruit may call a coach on the phone at any time during her high school career. If the coach is in the office and answers, the two are permitted to have a conversation. The coach, however, is *not* permitted to make (or return) calls to prospective riders until after July 1 of the student's senior year of high school – so if you get his or her voice mail and you aren't a senior yet, don't expect a call back.

Your best option for a first contact with coaches is to go online and fill out the program's prospective athlete questionnaire. Juniors should always begin their conversation with an equestrian team by taking this initial step, but if you want to be more personal and direct in your communication with the teams that are of the most interest to you, coaches are allowed to return emails to you after September 1 of your junior year so you may also reach out by direct email. Just remember to keep the messages brief and word them professionally. Direct emails can be used to send your resume materials and video links, as well as to ask specific questions about the team or program that have come up as a result of your preliminary research. Chatty, conversational emails with no real purpose won't demonstrate to the coach that you're an organized and mature candidate who deserves his or her full attention in the recruiting process.

If you're out at a show or clinic and see an NCEA coach observing the riders present, don't be offended if they don't make contact with you or even go so far as to walk the other way if they recognize you. The rules state that they may not approach you in an off-campus setting until after July 1 of your senior year and no coach wants to risk an NCAA infraction by chatting with a student who hasn't yet become a senior in the eyes of the organization.

(**Author's Note:** Contact rules may change shortly after the publication of this book. Refer to the current edition of the *Guide for the College-Bound Student Athlete* for details.)

Why all the regulations? For equestrian sports and for all college athletics, having a rigid structure in place gives each coach and each athletic program an equal opportunity to recruit top students and top athletes to come to their schools each year. Likewise, it prevents the programs that possess bigger recruiting budgets from gaining an unfair advantage over rival schools that have less funds to work with. Just as the horse draw at intercollegiate horse shows helps to level the playing field for riders who might not have access to the best mounts, the rules that govern NCAA athletics levels the playing fields for the teams within the organization.

One thing that the rules don't influence, however, is a school's recruiting approach, which often springs out of its greater campus culture or from a coach's individual philosophy. As a result, you might discover that the different programs you have an interest in all take slightly different approaches to the recruiting process. (Because the coaches' duties are numerous and intercollegiate equestrian is a year-round sport that takes place during both the fall *and* spring semesters, each one has his or her own preferred methods and schedule for contacting recruits and for discerning which ones will be the best additions to the team.)

Though it's a possibility that coaches might find you at a national or regional show, through an organized showcase or recruiting event or through published horse show results, there's a far better chance that *you* will need to reach out first and recruit the team in order to convince the coach to recruit you. If a survey and letter of interest arrive in your mail at the conclusion of your sophomore or beginning of your junior year, you'll know that a coach has put you on his or her radar already, but if you don't receive such information, the colleges most likely do not know about you and you'll need to approach the coaches from the schools on your list. The online athletic prospect form is *always* the first step you should take and at the same time you submit that information to the equestrian coaching staff, you should also take the time to fill out an interest form on the web page of the admissions office so that the institution may begin to contact you about academics and student life. (At many universities, the equestrian staff and admissions office don't regularly cross-compare their lists of interested students, so never assume that just because the riding coach knows of your interest that the admissions office does as well.)

If you prefer to communicate offline, you may send a formal letter of introduction and interest to the equestrian team as opposed to filling out the web form. In the letter, state the specific reason (or reasons) for your interest in their program, your goals for your college career (share both your academic and riding goals), give the name of your regular trainer (leave out any one with whom you've only taken clinics unless you've ridden in clinics with the same trainer more than twice per year in successive years), and include a one page resume of your academic and riding career highlights. (The packet should be no more than two pages in total – coaches who have an interest in learning more about you after reading the information will let you know.)

When coaches begin to respond to your inquiries, the first thing they'll want to see is video footage of you riding. It isn't important that your video look as though Steven Spielberg himself directed it (video shot by your parents, your trainer, or a friend is just fine), but it is crucial that the content be not only an accurate representation of your skills and abilities, but also that the footage is clean and doesn't include any elements that will detract from your presentation. It's also vital that your recruitment video be *short* – no longer than five minutes – because coaches know very quickly what they're looking for and don't have the luxury of extra time to slog through hours of footage. NCEA coaches receive hundreds of videos each year and will view them at a fairly rapid pace that won't allow for them to appreciate your superior editing skills or the attention to detail you paid when you attached your horse's fake tail that morning.

If you're putting together a riding recruitment video, adhere to the following guidelines:

- **Open with your best footage.** If you nailed down a tough equitation round at Harrisburg last fall, lead with that round in your video. Don't be afraid to show the entire course (coaches worry you've edited out something really bad if you have sudden gaps or cuts in it), but when you're working within a short time frame, don't waste it on footage that's only "okay." Coaches want to see that you have the ability to plan and execute a good strategy for your jumping rounds or horsemanship patterns so show those talents off as soon as you can. If your highlight at the last show was the counter canter to the trot fence and then you halted and backed up flawlessly, make sure that's in there too!

- **Add variety.** Because intercollegiate competition requires that you be comfortable on various kinds of horses, your video should include footage of you on more than one mount. Two is ideal for such a short video but three is okay if you don't have to make too many quick cuts to fit everything in. Perhaps you demonstrate a horsemanship pattern on an Arabian and then a Paint or show footage of you jumping a Thoroughbred, then include jumping footage of you on your trainer's big-bodied warmblood. It's also important to show your talents both on the flat and over fences (if you're a hunt seat rider) or on the rail and in patterns (if you're a western rider). You should include any unique abilities you have (riding in multiple disciplines, etc.) Finally hunt seat riders should remember to include some work without stirrups!

- **Don't edit too much.** Even though the video is short, don't make your cuts too choppy, but instead make sure that all of your edited pieces flow together. For example, you shouldn't show your approach to one fence, the jump and landing, and then cut with no warning to a different horse in a different location that shows you practicing sitting trot with no stirrups. Instead, allow the coaches to follow your video in a logical progression by showing several fences in a row so that you can demonstrate your eye for distances. For western riders, show coaches the big circle to small circle and lead change section of your reining pattern. But by the same token, don't linger too long on the horse at the walk or on a particularly long approach to a fence – you don't want to waste time on footage that doesn't show a specific skill.
- **Don't be afraid of imperfection.** While you certainly want the coaches to see you ride at your very best and minimize the amount of mistakes you make in the video, you also want to show that you're someone capable of learning and making improvements. If you approach a gymnastic and chip to the first element on your first pass but nail the timing on your second approach and sail through flawlessly, don't be afraid to show that improvement to your potential coaches if you feel that it shows one of your particularly strong moments.
- **Keep it neat and tidy.** You don't necessarily have to use show footage for your entire video (though it looks professional on the screen). If you have good clinic or schooling footage that demonstrates what you can do, you can use it alongside your show footage as long as you feel that you have presented your best self in all areas. If schooling footage is something you select, however, you should be properly attired for your discipline in neat and clean clothing and your horse should be properly turned out. For hunt seat riders, make sure your ponytail is tucked

into your helmet and your breeches and boots are relatively clean. For western riders, don't wear your ripped jeans and make sure that your hair is neatly contained as well. Safety helmets are allowed and encouraged for all disciplines.

- **Identify yourself at the beginning and the end.** Most video editing software makes it relatively easy to insert captions and credits at the beginning and end of your video and you should take advantage of that for this project. Make sure that your name is clearly spelled out, along with your high school name, your graduation year, and your contact information (email and phone number). Don't use an artsy font that may be hard to read onscreen; Arial or Times New Roman are standard fonts for a reason. Make sure the information appears at both the beginning *and* the end of the video for the coaches' convenience and don't be afraid to split the information onto two or three slides if it looks overwhelming on one.

- **Avoid distractions within the video.** Even though it might not look or sound right to you if your recruitment video doesn't feature a soundtrack with your favorite One Direction song blaring from the speakers, the coaches will appreciate the opportunity to watch the video without it. Background noise from the horse show or clinic is just fine as long as any people talking near the microphone aren't too loud or offensive.

(**Author's Note:** Parents, this includes any and all commentary that you might have on your daughter's ride. Saying "I'm so glad she didn't forget the course like she did last week" near the microphone isn't the best way to present your child to a coach who needs her to remember every course *every* time!) And though iPhones and iPads make shooting video on the spot easy and convenient for even the non-tech savvy, it's incredibly difficult to assess riders who appear on videos that constrain the action within two narrow black frames. As such, make sure that your video is shot with the device held horizontally or else use only footage from a regular video camera.

Once your video is complete, upload it to YouTube or another video sharing site, as this will allow you to quickly and easily email a link to the coaches who request video footage from you. As a backup, you can also burn a copy to a DVD that can be mailed or handed to coaches during campus visits. Some coaches have preferences as to what format the video arrives in and others don't care as long as the video is clear and arrives promptly.

Coaches who have strong interest in recruiting you may read your resume and watch your video, then invite you to campus either for an official or unofficial visit. (See Chapter Six for a full explanation of each.) If it's possible, they may also invite you to come to a meet and watch the team in action. If you are able to attend a meet, it's important to realize that events are hectic and the students from the host school are not only competing, but often are also responsible for helping tack up, untack, and move horses around as part of ensuring that the show runs smoothly. Coaches will likewise be engaged in making sure that their team has everything they need in order to compete successfully against their opponent, so your opportunities to ask in-depth questions and have them answered will be limited. As a result, at the competition, don't expect too much one-on-one time with anyone from the program, but instead take the time to carefully observe everything, from the way the format works to the way students are coached and the way teammates interact with each other.

If you're able to visit during a slower period (not during a meet) and are afforded the opportunity to meet one on one with coaches or with current team members, prepare your questions in advance to help you focus and make the best use of your time. Common questions you might ask are:

- How often a week does the team practice?
- At what time of day are practices?
- How do practices work in with students' academic schedules?
- What are the team's strength and conditioning requirements?
- What other regulations would I have to follow as a member of this team?

- How often does the team travel to away meets and how often does the team host home meets?
- What does a normal school day look like for a member of this team?
- Who is responsible for caring for the team's horses?
- What can I do right now to make myself a good candidate for this team?
- When do you hold your team tryouts and what is the tryout format?
- If I am selected for this team, how likely is it that I will compete in a show as a freshman? As a sophomore, junior, or senior?

The final question is one that is very important to ask because it will help inform you as to what role you would be expected to play for the team. NCEA equestrian teams are made up (on average) of forty-six team members but meets only require a minimum of four riders from each team (per event) to participate, so very often the number of competing riders per team is only eight or nine. The other riders all practice, help care for the horses, support the team, and are available to fill in (or move up) when necessary, but aren't the "first string" members and are more likely to do the equestrian equivalent of sitting the bench. You should therefore ask the coach how he or she sees you fitting into the team in the next year or in the next few years. The answer to the question will reveal whether or not your personal goals are a match for the ones that the program will have for you.

In examining your opportunities to get to know a particular coach and program, it's also important to ask the coach about attending a summer training camp (or you can check the team web site for information about it). Most NCEA riding programs offer a summer camp that are often open to all interested high school students. (Not everyone is recruited directly from these camps, as they are designed first and foremost to generate revenue and publicity for the program itself.) The length of the camps can vary anywhere from one weekend (two days) to a three or four day intensive program. The majority of the camps don't require students to provide their own horses but instead are held at college or university equestrian facilities with overnight housing for students provided on campus in residence halls. Camp dates tend to be set in late winter and slots begin to open up in the middle part of March each year so if you're interested in attending a camp, you'll need to plan ahead if you want to guarantee yourself a spot.

If you are able to visit campus, meet the coach and team members, and then decide that you have found the right school for you – and if the admissions office has accepted your application (they *always* have the final say in recruiting matters) - you may choose to make a verbal commitment to the program, which is simply a spoken agreement between you and the coach that you intend to enroll in the fall. If you are offered a riding scholarship by the program, you will also be asked to sign a **National Letter of Intent (NLI).** The NLI is a binding agreement between you and the college or university that commits you to attend that school for a period of two semesters (or three quarters, depending on the structure of the school's academic calendar). The school likewise commits to offering you athletic aid and agrees to cover all of your training and competition costs for that same period; the NLI only needs to be signed only once but is only good for one year. The coach determines whose scholarships will be renewed each year and you will be eligible for renewal as long as you remain in good athletic, academic, and social standing with the school. Having a one-year agreement also affords you the opportunity to transfer to a new school later if you choose.

If you verbally commit to one school early in the season, you are permitted under NCAA regulations to sign the NLI with a different program if they offer you a scholarship later and you change your mind about where you would like to enroll; it is, however, best to be proactive and up front in your communication of this change of situation with all coaches involved should you choose to do so. (You never know when poor conduct might come back to haunt you later if you don't!)

If you have already signed the NLI with one school but later wish to transfer your allegiance to a different school, you cannot officially transfer (as an equestrian) unless you are officially released from the school that holds your NLI. The letter is a legally binding contract between both you and the university and isn't a prospect to be undertaken lightly.

Students and parents should also realize that NCEA member colleges and universities are not necessarily the only ones with a formal recruiting process. In fact, many schools that compete under the umbrella of the IHSA have well-established recruitment practices that you will need to familiarize yourself with if you want your best chance at becoming a team member. (There are also a handful of NCEA-member schools that choose not to compete in the NCEA's head-to-head format but instead compete exclusively within the IHSA. These NCEA/IHSA hybrid schools are, however, also limited to an all-female team.)

Though the recruitment process within IHSA-member schools are not subject to the same rigorous rules as those within the NCEA, you most likely will find a substantial amount of overlap and might find yourself completing some of the same tasks during the recruitment process. Notable similarities between the two are coaches' requests for:

- **Completed prospective athlete questionnaires.** All coaches have their own unique methods for tracking their recruits, but the one thing they all have in common is that they begin the process with a prospect questionnaire. This form is available online through the team's web site.
- **Videos.** Coaches can't be everywhere and watch every recruit ride in person, so they all rely on video footage to show them what you can do.
- **Your resume/bio and a letter of introduction.** Both should be short. Remember, no more than one page for the letter and no more than one page for the resume. Your goal is to tell the coach who you are, when you'll graduate, where you currently go to school, your regular trainer's name (don't name drop with a list of famous clinicians), your academic interests, and the reason you want to go to

his or her school. On the resume, list only your biggest highlights and accomplishments.

As long as you have these three items ready to go for all of the programs that interest you (whether NCEA, IHSA, or a combination of the two), you will have all of the materials you need to begin making contacts and learning more about the schools on your list. As you begin to receive responses from various programs, if will help keep you organized if you maintain a file folder (either physically or online) for each individual school where you can store the feedback and materials you receive from each school. You should also track your own communicative efforts and record your thoughts regarding each program. Your files can also be a handy place to jot down questions about a particular school as they come to mind so that you will remember to ask them when the opportunity presents itself.

A few final notes regarding the recruitment process for intercollegiate equestrian teams:

- **At the college level, most two- and three-sport athletes must choose to compete in only one – including equestrians.** If you currently play basketball in the winter and ride in the spring summer and fall, you'll have to make a choice when you get to college. Varsity and even many club-level equestrian coaches will expect your total commitment as a student athlete, just as varsity basketball and swimming coaches expect the same from their team members. Intercollegiate equestrian competitions run year-round (in both fall and spring semesters) and it isn't fair to the equestrian team if you have to miss half of the meets because you're away with the soccer or softball team. Riding in college is a team sport and you'll need to be one hundred percent committed to your team if you want to participate.
- **Like any other college sport, it isn't unusual for coaches to change programs over the summer – so the coach who recruits you in the spring may not necessarily be the one you try out with in the fall.** For this reason (and

many others), it's absolutely crucial that you select your college based on more reasons than simply the equestrian program so that your school experience can be as well-balanced as possible. (Your allegiance, after all, should be first to your academic goals and the school, not to a coach – even if he or she did actively recruit you into the program.) It's also important that you enter your college riding career with an open mind and coach-able attitude because every new coach has something to teach you and it's up to you to find out what that is, no matter the circumstance.

- **Any student can be a candidate for a college equestrian team, regardless of their previous competitive history.** Though riders with impressive riding resumes are normally at the forefront of the recruitment process for NCEA coaches, talented walk-ons who make their presence known both with their skill, determination, and a team player attitude have an opportunity to earn a spot as well. You might not get a scholarship offer and you might not be the team standout whom they publish press releases about, but you can still have a wonderful college riding career. (And remember that in the IHSA, having less prior competitive experience can even work to your advantage!)

- **The college admissions office is the one that confirms whether or not you can get in to the school, not the coach.** It's not unheard of for coaches to say a lot of things when they're in the process of talking up a talented student. Some might even make verbal promises that their school can't keep. The majority of them don't do it with any malicious intent – they're simply so enthusiastic about their teams that their mouths get ahead of them. They're also very busy individuals, so it's your responsibility to ensure that you follow through on the application process in a timely fashion (see Chapter Eight) and that you consult closely with the admissions office to determine your chances of admission before you take a coach's word as a firm contract. Some well-established coaches do have a degree of influence over a student's admissibility, but you should never count on it as a guarantee or use it as an excuse to relax your academic standards.

- **Riding scholarships are not available to all riders from all schools.** Scholarships and financial aid will be addressed fully in Chapter Nine.
- **The number one factor that *all* coaches want in a rider on their team is a great attitude. Period.** No matter how talented a rider is and no matter how many awards she's received, a coach spends far too much time with his or her riders – practicing at home, traveling to and from competitions, and at the meets themselves – to want to spend a lot of time with someone who walks through the door every day with a bad attitude. It's important in return that you make sure to show up (on time) to every meeting, tryout, practice, and show with a smile on your face and a ready-to-learn, willing-to-help, team player sensibility. Assist with the little things – setting fences or putting out cones, grooming horses after practice, or even boosting team morale – and your coach will always appreciate having you around.

If you are one of the lucky ones chosen to represent your college or university as a member of the equestrian team and you go in ready to dedicate yourself to the group, you will have a wonderful and fulfilling college experience and make lifelong friends. What's more, you'll graduate with unbelievable (but true!) stories from your travels with the team, inside jokes that only your teammates understand, and a sense of belonging that very few riders have an opportunity to feel in what is otherwise a very individually-driven sport. It's a wonderful thing and far more valuable than a lot of ribbons hanging on your wall - though you might also earn more than your fair share of those along the way!

8
WILL BEING AN EQUESTRIAN INCREASE MY CHANCE OF BEING ADMITTED?

"Going into college I did not want to ride on a team or get overly involved in the equestrian program, as I wanted to branch out and attempt being a "normal" person."
Brittany, IDA dressage alumna

Even though most high school students believe that fall of senior year is the time they should begin to work on their applications for college, if you feel as though you have a solid list of colleges and universities that you're excited about and you believe that each of them could be a good fit, it's not out of the question to begin assembling a few pieces of your application during the spring of your junior year. This is also usually the time that your high school guidance counselors will begin to send passes for you to come and meet with them to discuss your college plans or will hold formal class meetings, so with a solid college list and "plan of attack" for applying, you'll be able to maximize the time you spend in the counseling office. Because senior year is usually rather academically challenging and is also a socially busy time in your life, you'll also prevent a lot of stress if you are able to get ahead of the game. You'll also find that, if you put a little effort in early, the time freed up by just that little bit of pre-planning is a wonderful pay off during your senior year. If you're particularly organized, you may be able to complete as many as five of the six components of your college applications before senior year even begins!

In this chapter, the six primary components of a college application that will be examined are:

- **The application itself.** Today, the majority of college applications are filed online, either through a college or university's own online form, via the Common Application web site, or by using the Universal College Application (all of which will be addressed later in this chapter).
- **Your official high school transcript.** This record of all of your high school courses, grades, and other information that is specific to you must be sent to the colleges directly from your high school guidance office. (Your *unofficial* transcript was mentioned in Chapter Five and should be accessible for you to view at any time.) The transcript must display your school's official (raised) seal to be considered official.
- **Essay(s).** Though some colleges don't request that you write essays for admission, many will require at least one and possibly two or more. You might also encounter requests for one longer essay and one or two short answer questions. Most essays are personal in nature and provide a chance for the admissions office to learn things about you that don't necessarily have to do with your academic performance. Essay requirements all have word limits so you'll need to be concise with your thoughts.
- **Standardized test scores.** Colleges will request official copies of your ACT or SAT test scores to be sent either from your high school or directly from the testing agency. Some colleges have gone "test optional," meaning that they don't take your test results into account when they decide whether or not to admit you – but even then, many of those colleges *will* require you to submit scores if you want to be considered for academic scholarship money.
- **Recommendation letter(s) or form(s).** Many colleges also want to hear from the people who know you in a professional capacity – teachers, coaches, counselors, etc. – to find out if they believe you will do well as a student at the college level. Some will require just one while others will want two or three. Through the Common Application or Universal College Application, recommendations are submitted through an online form that your recommenders

can access online; other schools, however, may prefer that an actual letter be sent from the person making the recommendation. In most cases, you will not be able to read recommendations beforehand and many application forms (namely the Common Application and Universal College Application) will make you waive your rights to reading them altogether.

- **Activities resume.** In order to get to know you better, schools will ask you to list your extracurricular activities and leadership positions so they can see what you do outside of class and how you will help shape life on their campus. Normally you will be asked to submit this information on a section of the application web form, but some colleges will request that you upload a resume document that outlines your extracurricular activities (sports, leadership, volunteering, church, etc.). In addition to what types of activities you participate in, admissions officers also want to know how many hours per week you spend on each one, so do the math ahead of time if you can. (Estimates are fine if you don't know exactly or if your time commitments vary.)

The six parts of a college application are each important in their own right, though most college admissions officials will say that a student's academic record (including the difficulty and rigor of courses taken), their essays, and test scores tend to be scrutinized the most carefully during the review process. But each part reveals a part of you, so none of them should be glossed over or hurried through as you prepare your applications.

Though you can work on essays and organize your resume items at just about any time during junior year, taking either the SAT or the ACT requires more advanced scheduling and preparation. Both tests are designed to measure students' aptitude in certain key areas and both have an optional essay section, but there are some clear differences between the tests as well. In fact, the majority of colleges and universities will accept either test from applicants, so many students decide to take both tests at least once in order to see which one they perform better on.

The most common questions asked by students in regard to testing are:

- **Which test should I take?** Colleges and universities generally recognize the ACT and SAT equally - though in a few particular cases, a specific test is required. If your potential colleges don't have a preference, don't be swayed by cafeteria gossip that says one test is easier than the other. (There's no scientific proof that indicates this is the case.) Instead, if you are a fast reader and you are fairly consistent in all of your school subjects, the ACT can be a good fit. Conversely, the SAT emphasizes problem solving and reasoning skills, so if you're slightly more intuitive, that can be a good choice. Evaluate your PSAT or PLAN scores from earlier in your high school career if you have them – the PSAT is the precursor to the SAT and the PLAN is the precursor to the ACT. Both are used as indicators for your projected SAT or ACT score and your school counselor, a trusted teacher, or an educational consultant should be able to help you interpret the results.
- **When should I test for the first time?** It's recommended that high school students not take the test before December or January of their junior year. In most cases, students wait until March or April and then test for a second time in May or June. Depending on a student's testing abilities (namely, whether he or she has test anxiety or a learning disorder that requires accommodations during testing), a guidance counselor or teacher should be able to recommend the best timing for a particular individual. (A few states also use the ACT as their state's educational progress evaluation and will administer it to all of the junior class free of charge in the spring.)
- **How many times should I take the test?** Again, the answer to this question depends on the individual student. Good test takers or students with very high aptitude may only need to test once while others may need to sit for the test two or three times to achieve a personal best. It's important for students to know before they sit down to take the test if they will be applying to schools who take the

highest overall test score from one sitting or if they will "super score" (e.g. give the best possible composite score from all sittings). If a student plans to apply to both types of school, then multiple sittings might still be in his or her best interest. A student's score typically plateaus after the third sitting, however, so fourth or fifth attempts are not recommended.

- **Should I take a test preparation course?** Nervous test takers can benefit from strategies to help them relax and focus on the test, but strong test takers can also benefit from learning tips and tricks ahead of time to help them maximize their results. There may be test preparation companies or private tutors located within your city or region who can help; alternatively, online programs (which include practice test sessions) can be found through both testing companies and private entities. Beginning with the 2016 SAT, free online preparation will be available through the Khan Academy, which has partnered with the College Board. Outside of Khan Academy, some other online preparation services are free but others charge a fee, the amount of which can vary widely. Research thoroughly before you commit to any preparatory program.

- **Do I need to take SAT subject tests? (And what if I take the ACT?)** Specific programs at some schools (e.g. schools of engineering, foreign language majors, etc.), will require you to submit the scores from an SAT subject test in addition to your general SAT or ACT. You don't necessarily have to use the SAT as your primary test if you plan to take an SAT subject test (sometimes referred to as the SAT II), however; you may take the ACT as your entrance exam and then take the SAT II for your required subject. And even if it's not a requirement of your intended college major, you might consider taking the SAT II to help you demonstrate proficiency in a specific area if the school you're applying to is particularly competitive for admission – especially if your classroom grades don't demonstrate this as clearly as you would like.

(**Author's Note:** For students applying to schools in the

Ivy League and other highly selective schools, the SAT II
is often required in order to help the admissions committees
discern between highly-qualified applicants. Read their
web sites carefully for details and guidelines.)

There are also varying schools of thought regarding when and
how you should submit your standardized test scores to the
colleges to which you will apply. This decision can be further
challenging for financially aware students because there is no fee
to send up to four copies of your test results directly from the
testing company if you request it at the time you take the test; if,
however, you wait until your score is released and ask the
company to send it at that time, a fee is charged. (Some students
may qualify for a fee waiver for both taking the test and for having
it sent; your guidance counselor can help you determine if you
qualify.) Though SAT has developed a "Score Choice" option that
allows for some flexibility in evaluating your scores before you
decide whether to send them or not, students should meet with a
counselor, a teacher, or talk with their parents prior to the test date
to determine what the best plan for them will be. (If you've visited
campuses and have contact information for your admissions
counselors, you may also contact them for insight.)

**If you plan to register with the NCEA (NCAA) Eligibility
Center as a prospective equestrian athlete, remember that you
must report all scores to them directly at the time of testing;
there is no other option.**

Once your testing strategy is firmly in place, you might move
on to consideration of potential essay topics during the spring of
your junior year. In some cases, your English or composition
teacher might assign a college admission essay as a writing project
using actual test prompts to get you started. If that isn't the case,
however, many prompts become available in late February or early
March to give you plenty of time to perfect what you want to say.
In particular, the Common Application and Universal College
Application – both of which are nationally-recognized application
services that allow one "common" or "universal" application to be
filled out by a student who wishes to send it to multiple schools –

are known for releasing their essay topics early in the spring.

Drafting your initial essay before summer vacation is ideal, not only because it affords you plenty of time to brainstorm what you would like to write about, but it also means that you're still seeing your teachers every day and can solicit their feedback on your progress. In particular, English and social studies teachers will already be familiar with your writing and able to give supportive critiques as your essay takes shape. An early start will also help you go through the writing process while your mind is still sharp and in "school" mode before summer and a full schedule of riding lessons and horse shows consume your daily life. **Be careful not to allow too many readers to influence you, however, as this strategy can often lead to unnecessary confusion. Don't over-edit your essay either; write one or two drafts in the spring, put it away for summer, then re-visit it again in the fall before you add it to your application.**

As an equestrian, you may choose to use the essay section to talk about your sport and what it means to you. Doing so can be a fantastic addition to your application and not only reveal your personality, but also your inner character to the admissions committee. Horses have a way of shaping students into organized, thoughtful, and worldly people - and what better opportunity to display that side of you than in your personal essay? What's more, your participation in equestrian sports can sometimes serve as a "hook" in the admissions process – that is, something that makes you stand apart from the other applicants and can give you an edge if the admissions process grows selective. (After all, riding isn't a sport that everyone has access to at their high school or even has an interest in; by showing how it's opened doors for you and shaped you as a person, you can easily demonstrate how you will bring this experience with you to campus and become a leader in the student body.)

All students (equestrians and non-equestrians) must be careful to keep their essays on topic, however – and no matter how you interpret what the prompt says, that topic is **you**. A great college essay is one that tells the reader things about you that don't appear anywhere else in the application, so the first rule of thumb is not to rehash information the admissions staff can easily spot in your transcript. The essay is the place where your personality emerges and where the two dimensions of your grades and test scores suddenly become a three-dimensional individual with goals and an interesting life story. For example, on your activities list, you might have revealed that you're a competitive equestrian and that you also work part-time for your trainer mucking stalls or as a show groom. But those are just activities that you *do* – in the essay, you talk about how you *feel* when you're at the barn, what experiences you've had traveling to shows, and what winning and losing has taught you about yourself. You get to share your goals for the future and how you see riding playing a role in it. In fact, everything is pretty much fair game as long as you stay within the parameters of the essay prompt.

Though essays are relatively open-ended in terms of how you may respond to the prompts, they shouldn't be treated as a free-for-all either. In fact, there are some generally accepted guidelines you should be sure to adhere to:

- **Always stay on prompt.** View the prompt as a set of stocks like the ones your vet or farrier might use when working on your horse – it's the framework that keeps everything organized and prevents anything (in this case, your essay) from straying outside of a set area. The biggest mistake most students make is to begin the essay correctly on prompt (e.g. Who is your hero and why?) and then somewhere around the two hundred word mark, they stray off onto a tangent and lose the direction – and effectiveness – of the finished product.
- **Always talk about yourself.** Even if the essay prompt asks you to talk about your hero, it really wants to know more about *you* in relation to that person. Obviously you will want to introduce your hero at the beginning, but what the admissions office really wants to know as the essay goes on is how are *you* different because of that person you named? What inspires *you* about him or her? Remember – it's *your* college application and the essay needs to reflect that!

- **Avoid depressing topics when possible.** There's a chance that one of the biggest things that's happened in your life so far was a tragedy – the loss of a relative or friend, the loss of a favorite horse, the divorce of your parents, etc. But while overcoming adversity can make for a wonderful story and might well end on a positive note, it's hard to fit within a restrictive six hundred fifty word limit – and even harder to strike the appropriate tone while doing so. Unless you're very certain that you can pull it off and have a teacher or counselor to help guide you, avoid the really heart-wrenching topics if you can.

- **It's okay to be *under* the word limit.** If your essay stays on prompt, is descriptive, and says everything that you want to say in just five hundred words, don't feel compelled to cram an extra hundred and fifty words in just because you can. The best essays get right to the point and wrap up without rambling – and with the average admissions counselor spending less than two minutes reading each student's essay, shorter is better in most cases.

Perhaps you are an equestrian who chooses to avoid writing about your sport in the essay section because it features so prominently in your extracurricular resume or is mentioned frequently in your recommendations. Or maybe another story from your life fulfills one of the prompts better or you prefer to talk about riding in a short answer or supplemental essay (if it's required). There is no hard and fast rule about how you should talk about riding in your college application – or if you even need to at all! The goal of your entire college application is to paint an authentic picture of you as a person. It's a snapshot of you as you emerge from high school, so *you* are ultimately the one who decides what the finished picture will reveal to your prospective colleges.

Prospective equestrian team athletes (both varsity and club): Even if you have already been in contact with the coach while on a campus visit, at a recruiting event, or have filled out the athletic recruitment form online, you also need to check "equestrian" on the sports or athletics section of the

application so that both the admissions office and the equestrian program know of your continued interest. This allows them to properly track you in their database and also allows them to update the coach in regards to your admission status as acceptances begin to go out.

Many equestrians often fear writing about their sport because they worry that their activities resume is already too consumed with riding and riding-related activities and they don't want to appear too one-sided in the admissions process. Does this sound like you? Are you also worried that your resume isn't diverse enough to make you a good candidate for admission because riding – as time-consuming and enriching as it is – doesn't demonstrate enough of your skills to the committee?

To view the equestrian part of your resume as limiting your opportunities because it makes you look one-sided is to miss the opportunity to point out a lot of wonderful qualities, skills, and experiences the sport has brought into your life. Each one of those qualities can easily be explored and discussed within your resume.

Are you a student who has skipped over a lot of your high school's organized sports and clubs because you've dedicated the majority of your after-school hours to riding and spending time at the barn?

If so, your best strategy is to look at your extracurricular resume not as a listing of club and organization names, but instead as an inventory of your skills and abilities. For example, if working for your trainer has taught you how to get one horse ready for schooling at the exact moment that he steps off the one that needs cooling down *and* you've learned how to get the evening feed ready at the same time, take a moment to recognize the organizational skills you've developed. This is a skill that will make you a great college student.

Have you managed never to turn in a late homework assignment even after you missed a week of school for a competition?

Congratulations! You possess excellent time management skills that are also valuable for college students.

Are you the student at the barn upon whom your trainer relies to help other students get ready for their lessons or for their classes at shows?

If you are, you have tremendous leadership abilities that you need to showcase. Every campus is eager to find and develop the young people who will be leaders in business, politics, health, and all other areas of the working world and if you already have experience in that area, they're going to want you to come to their campus so that you can continue to develop your abilities.

Are you also a horse owner? Whether your horse lives in your backyard or is boarded somewhere, you're responsible for that animal's health and well-being. Perhaps your parents assist you in certain ways – either financially or maybe just through their guidance and support - but by the time you've acquired your driver's license, there's a good chance that you've taken a lot of the duties upon yourself. Maybe you're the one who decides what feed and supplements your horse receives, arranges his turnout regimen, and calls to schedule the vet and farrier when they're needed. As you commit your equestrian-specific extracurricular activities to paper, don't short change the unique things that riding and caring for horses have brought into your life and the way these experiences and opportunities have shaped you. Instead, use all of those skills to demonstrate why you're exactly the kind of student who will thrive in college!

The final piece of the application that requires consideration before your junior year ends is your letters of recommendation. Who you will ask to write them for you? What people are the most qualified to speak about your potential for success as a college student?

By timing your request for spring, you grant your recommenders a generous amount of time with which to compose their thoughts and to get the finished product submitted. In particular, if you plan to ask a very popular teacher from your high school to recommend you, realize that he or she will no doubt have a multitude of your classmates making the same request in the fall – so by asking in the spring, you ensure that your name is at the top of the list! You can also guarantee that you'll be able to receive recommendations from any teachers or counselors who might be on maternity leave or change jobs between school years – it's important that the recommendations come from those who really know you and you won't have time in the fall to get acquainted with a new counselor or teacher in time for them to write one for you.

It's also important that you have some idea what the person is going to say about you before you select your recommenders. It seems like a very obvious thing to do because you wouldn't automatically ask for support from a teacher with whom you had a bad experience or a coach who cut you from a team - yet sometimes a recommendation isn't as black and white as "I like this student" or "I don't like this student." Sometimes a teacher whom you feel that you know really well through his or her exciting history lectures might not actually know *you* well enough to comment on your character beyond "She got an A in world history and always turned her assignments in on time." Or perhaps you and your guidance counselor don't meet very often and therefore don't have enough of a working relationship for him to write a personal recommendation. If that's the case, he might only list your resume items and check a box that says "I do not know this student well enough to comment." Neither of those observations will necessarily *hurt* your chances of admission – but they aren't exactly glowing waves of support either.

For home-schooled students, the letter of recommendation or recommendation form can seem like an extra challenge to submit, as many schools request teacher recommendations and, though your parents might do an excellent job with your home school curriculum, they aren't allowed to comment on your application. If you fit into this category, first read the guidelines from the admissions offices at the schools to which you're applying. They might allow your riding coach or another home school parent (if you work within a home school group) serve as your recommender. Other good options include your pastor or minister, a tutor who has worked with you on test preparation or a particular subject, or someone you've worked or done volunteer service for.

If you manage to stay on top of your grades and the pieces of your application come together before the first day of your senior year of high school, all that will be left for you to complete will be the easy part: the application itself. The Common Application becomes available on August 1 each year and most colleges that don't use the Common Application or Universal College Application will have their application for the current year posted online between July 15 and August 15. (Check with the individual schools' web sites for the exact date so you can make sure that you're filling out the correct version, as applications often change slightly from year to year. You don't want to begin filling out the form too early because last-minute changes might make your application invalid and you'll need to start from scratch – a hassle that you don't want after you've already done so much strong preparation.)

Regardless of what application you use (Common, Universal, or school-specific), you will find that very standard questions will be asked, including your name, address, high school name, and Social Security or resident alien number (if you have your permanent visa or a Green Card). You'll also need to answer questions about your parents (their marital status, where they live, where they went to school, their occupations, etc.) and your siblings (their ages and where they currently go to school). Each school may have variations in the questions that they ask, but the majority of the information you'll need for one school is the same information you'll need for another. There is no need to fill the entire form out in one sitting either; with online applications, you'll set up an account on the university's web system that will allow you to go in and edit your application form as many times as you want to before you actually have to submit it. Later, your online account through the college's web portal will be the way you track whether or not all of your materials have arrived from your high school. The web portal might also be the way that you receive your admission decision and enrollment information (including housing forms and parking information), so it's crucial that you keep track of your username and password for each college and university that you send an application to.

The final choice you'll need to make regarding your college application is what type of decision you'd like to be considered for. There are four common options available – though not every school offers every option – and each one has advantages and disadvantages, so choose carefully.

- **Early Acceptance.** If you choose early acceptance, you will send your completed application to a school (or schools) by a fall deadline – usually in November or December – with the understanding that the school will notify you of their decision as early as they are able to. (Usually the notification arrives before Christmas or right after the New Year.) If the school accepts you, you are not required to attend and have the rest of senior year to decide. The advantage of early decision is simply to learn of your admissions result as soon as you can so that you can either commit to the school or plan to attend somewhere different.
- **Early Decision (I).** Early decision likewise has an early fall deadline that varies by institution – sometimes it's as early as the middle of October and sometimes it isn't until the first of December. The main idea behind early decision is that if a school is your first choice and admits you in their first round of decisions, you will commit to attending in the fall and must rescind all of your other applications. Early decision applications are not to be taken lightly (as it's nearly impossible to change your mind after you've been admitted) but it can be advantageous if your first choice school is highly selective, as indicating your strong interest in them can result in their strong mutual interest in you.
- **Early Decision (II).** A second wave of early decision applications are usually due just after the New Year for schools that offer this option. (January 2 through January 15 are common deadlines.) This gives you a little more time to decide if you'd like to commit yourself to a particular school for the next four years or it can give you a

chance to commit to a second-choice school if your first choice school doesn't admit you earlier in the fall.

- **Regular decision.** The most common application approach is regular decision, which means that whenever your application and supplementary materials arrive at the school and are reviewed, you won't learn of their decision until spring (usually mid-March, but sometimes not until early April). If it's a school that you and your counselor are confident that you will be admitted to, it's fine to wait – though you'll have more time in the spring to make your final decision if you choose an early acceptance option (if it's available).

You might also apply to some colleges and universities who adhere to a **rolling admissions** policy; that is, the admissions staff evaluates applications as they come in (on a "rolling" basis) and generally respond to students with a decision within a few weeks. If you apply to schools with rolling admissions policies early in the application cycle (prior to December 1 of your senior year), you can give yourself at least four months to gather more information about the colleges by visiting and researching their programs before you have to make your final decision and send an enrollment deposit.

Once your application file is complete and has been reviewed by one or more members of the admissions staff, the college will make one of four decisions regarding your application status:

- **Acceptance.** Your application has been approved and you may join the student body on campus next fall if you want to. Normally included with your acceptance packet is a deadline by which you must tell them "yes" or "no" (usually May 1 of your senior year) and information regarding things you will need to know about if you plan to enroll, like financial aid and freshman housing.
- **Denial.** The school will not have a place for you in the fall. Though being denied from a school – especially if it's your first choice – can be a devastating experience, it's important not to take the decision personally. They didn't

reject *you* specifically, but rather your criteria for application; each school sets institutional goals for their enrollment division every year and applicants either match the profile or they don't. In some years, the school may want to increase their out-of-state student population; in other years, they may need more trumpets in the band or forwards on the basketball team. If you didn't fit the parameters at one school, however, chances are you did at several others.

- **Deferral.** Common among schools with Early Decision options, a deferral is the school's way of saying that they don't want to accept or deny you in their early round of selection. Instead, they will delay making a decision about your application until they evaluate the rest of the early files; they might also request to see updated grades or test scores before you're re-evaluated. You will receive a final decision notification later - usually in the spring. It's important if you are deferred from your first choice school that you reach out to the admissions office to let them know that and express your strong continued interest. Work closely with your college counselor to outline a strategy that will help you get accepted in that second round. (Deferrals can still end in denial - but savvy proactive students can help themselves avoid this fate!)

- **Wait List.** A wait list decision is the equivalent of admission decision limbo. Being wait-listed means that the school will allow you to enroll in the fall if space becomes available, but being on a school's waitlist is a tenuous place to be. There are never any guarantees of a spot opening up and if a space *does* become available to you, it's often long after other colleges have filled their freshman classes. Thus, if you're on the waitlist at your first choice school, your best option is to follow through with the enrollment process at your second choice, as you won't necessarily have another option if the waitlist at your first choice doesn't open up after all.

One other far less common admission decision that is sometimes seen from very large universities is that of **deferred**

enrollment. With deferred enrollment, the school accepts you, but does not allow you to enroll in the fall. Instead, you must wait until the second semester begins (January) to arrive on campus – leaving you with nothing to do in August when the rest of your friends leave for their colleges. Deferred enrollment can be an option for students who want to spend time on the fall horse show circuit and for whom a midyear start will be no big deal from a social standpoint. For other students, however, who need a supportive orientation environment with their freshman classmates before jumping right into classes on campus, a deferred enrollment can harm their chances of success in college.

Finally, one of the most common questions that equestrians and their parents want to know when it comes to the college application process – especially when the student hopes to join a varsity equestrian team – is whether or not the coach has any influence on the student's ability to get admitted. Because equestrian is not a head count sport like football or basketball that brings revenue into the school, the answer really varies based on the institution. In particular, for schools that offer riding scholarships and the schools with teams that are recognized through the athletic department, the coach might be able to reach out to the admissions office on behalf of a student and share information that can help that student gain admission. But for the majority of schools (even for those schools with NCEA and IHSA varsity teams), the students have to have the right grades, scores, well-written essays, and recommendations to be admitted, regardless of their abilities in the saddle. If a student has researched potential schools carefully and matched his or her academic profile to that of the school before submitting an application (as discussed in Chapter Four), then the influence of a coach should not be required to address the student's admission status in the first place. The student should be fully capable of obtaining admission based on his or her own merits.

It's an exciting day when your first college acceptance letter arrives and you deserve a round of excited celebration after your hard work has paid off. Don't think for a moment, however, that your job is over once you've been admitted to colleges. Admission is certainly an accomplishment, but it isn't the only challenge before you on your journey to college. You'll still have to work through how to pay for your education and prepare to move to campus.

9

I'M ACCEPTED! WHAT SCHOLARSHIPS ARE AVAILABLE TO ME AND WILL I BE ELIGIBLE FOR FINANCIAL AID?

"Apply for as many scholarships as you can find and spend a few hours a week looking for scholarships. Be persistent and creative looking for scholarships." **Kate, IHSA western alumna**

The cost of college – as well as who in your family will be responsible for it – was addressed in Chapter Four when you began your initial college search. As you work through the application process and begin to receive acceptance notifications, however, the idea of writing a significant check to cover your tuition, room, and board becomes an impending reality for both you and your parents! Some of your acceptance letters might arrive with scholarship awards included, while others might require a separate scholarship application, essay, tryout, or interview if you want to receive full consideration for receiving them. Then there are the schools that might offer no scholarship aid whatsoever and instead will recommend that you fill out financial aid forms to see if the government (state or federal) or the school itself can offer grant or loan aid to help reduce your cost of attendance. This chapter will examine these options and how they can be used to fund your college education.

The first option – and the one that is viewed the most favorably among students and their parents alike – is a **scholarship.** A scholarship is a sum of money that the school awards to you based on specific criteria that they have set, such as your academic abilities (grades and test scores), athletic talents (including riding), or artistic skills (including music, the visual arts, dance, or theatre). Most scholarships likewise have conditions attached to them that you must adhere to while you are enrolled in college – usually a grade point average you must meet or exceed each semester (in the case of academic scholarships). Students on any form of scholarship are also required to remain in good academic standing with the school, which means that you must not cheat on exams, violate an Honor Code agreement, or break any other university rules. Some scholarships are **renewable**, which means that as long as you continue to meet the required criteria, you will receive the scholarship each year that you are enrolled. Others are only for one year and you will be responsible for making up the amount of the scholarship after that.

Many of the colleges and universities to which you will apply will have scholarships that are available to freshman students and it will be your responsibility during your application process to find out what you will need to do in order to be considered. Many schools will simply use your application for the college itself as your application for scholarship but others will not. Visit the admissions office page on the web site of each of your schools to learn what scholarships might be a fit for you and, if necessary, follow up with an admissions counselor to make sure that you have done everything necessary to fulfill the requirements. If there is a special date on which scholarship applicants must come to campus to take a test, submit to an interview, or perform in an audition or tryout, mark it on your calendar as early as possible so that you don't schedule anything else for that date. (Colleges and universities traditionally don't allow make up scholarship interviews or auditions, so you'll need to make the commitment to attend on the date the school has selected. If it's particularly difficult for you to travel a long distance to be at the school on that date, find out if they will allow a Skype or phone interview.)

Contrary to the urban myths that are often thrown around, the most substantial scholarship money you will be eligible for will come directly from the college or university itself. Though major corporations and organizations get media attention by offering large amounts of scholarship money each year, in most cases you're just as likely to purchase a winning lottery ticket to pay for school as you are to win that type of scholarship. Instead, for additional scholarship resources, look closer to home. Sit down with your parents and make a list of all of the organizations that you and they belong to – including (and especially!) any national and regional equestrian groups that you have a membership with. The United States Pony Club, the United States Equestrian Federation, and other national governing bodies all have scholarships available to junior members, as do many state horsemen's associations and groups. After the equestrian organizations, don't forget to include your church and community groups, local companies and financial organizations (banks and credit unions that are local or regional), and your own high school. You should also check with your parents' employers if they work outside the home – some companies reserve scholarship money for the children of employees and you may be eligible.

As you research outside scholarships through community and organizations, it is worth noting that you'll need to consult closely with the college you ultimately plan to attend to make sure that they will accept all of the awards you bring to them and not retract any of their own award dollars if you reach a certain amount. This is because most merit awards from the colleges and universities themselves are not awarded to you in actual currency, but instead arrive in the form of a tuition discount. In other words, the college "discounts" your tuition in the amount of the scholarship award each year that you receive it. Pending the evaluation of your family's financial aid application forms by the school, you might see a reduction in school, state, or federal aid if you are "over-awarded" with external money because each school tries to balance its income numbers for the members of the first year class as a means to build its annual operating budget. Tuition revenue is what keeps schools open for business and no college or university wants to come up short of their projected budget number each year.

If you believe that your external scholarships will cause you to be an over-awarded student, contact the organizations who have offered you scholarships and find out if the scholarship money can be used for room and board costs, for books, or can be held for a semester or a year when you might have more need of it. Some schools will be willing to work with you and others will have more rigid policies.

Athletic scholarships are, of course, the ultimate dream for every competitive student athlete - from football players to equestrians - and they certainly can help to make a college education more affordable than it may otherwise be. As has been mentioned previously in this book, however, it's extremely rare to earn a full ride scholarship to college if you're an equestrian because it isn't a revenue-generating sport the way that football and basketball are. The majority of riding scholarships are nominal and some aren't even good for tuition payments but instead are restricted to helping cover the cost of your riding lessons and team practices. (Still, this type of scholarship can help keep your overall school expense down and means that you don't have to worry about coming up with your lesson funds each semester. Every little bit helps!)

If you are being recruited by a coach with the offer of a riding scholarship, it's important that you ask questions about the scholarship so that you can fully understand how the money will be put to work for you and what you will have to do in order to keep it. The last thing you want to do is get to school, have a great first semester or even a great first couple of years and then discover that you've lost your scholarship for one reason or another and can't afford to continue on to graduation. As such, be sure that you know the answers to the following questions:

- Is the scholarship renewable or is it restricted to one year?
- What requirements will I have to fulfill in order to renew my scholarship each year?
- In what situation(s) would I be in danger of losing my scholarship? (What if I become injured and can't ride for a semester?)
- If I am in danger of losing my scholarship, how and when will I be notified of this fact?
- Is there a certain date by which I need to commit (verbally or by signing) to the school in order to receive the scholarship?***

***The National Candidates' Reply Date for colleges and universities in the United States is always May 1 of the year in which you will enroll as a freshman. Schools that are members of the National Association for College Admission Counseling (NACAC) are required to abide by the organization's *Statement of Principles of Good Practice*, which states that schools may **not** pressure students into committing prior to May 1 (with the exception being students who have applied and been accepted through an Early Decision I or Early Decision II binding agreement). As such, coaches should **not** be able to pressure students to commit prior to May 1 – though they *may* award scholarships on a first-come, first-served basis.

Scholarships are not the only method through which you might receive "free" money to help pay for college, however; **grants** are also a form of student aid that can be awarded to students and do not need to be repaid after graduation. Grants can come from the college or university itself, your state government, the federal government, or even from an outside source. The majority of grants are awarded to students who demonstrate financial need on their financial aid application forms, though some may be awarded based on merit (similar to a scholarship).

The most common and most used financial aid application form that students and their families fill out each year to be considered for grant awards and for loans is the one produced by the federal government: The Free Application for Federal Student Aid (FAFSA). The FAFSA essentially takes a snapshot of your family's current financial situation based on the income tax filings of the previous year and uses that information to determine what your Expected Family Contribution (EFC) should be for your college tuition. The lower the EFC, the more aid a student can be eligible for. The higher the EFC, the less aid is presented by the colleges and universities, who all receive the exact same FAFSA data from the government and plug it into their own in-house awarding matrixes (similar to the FAFSA forecast and net price calculators that were mentioned in Chapter Four).

Just like with ACT and SAT scores, you select which colleges and universities you would like your FAFSA data sent to at the time at which you file. Unlike the ACT and SAT, however, the

FAFSA is entirely free and there is never a charge to send the information. If you find yourself on a web site that requires payment in order to submit your FAFSA information, you are not on the government site and should exit immediately.

The FAFSA is completed on or after January 1 of the year in which you will enroll in college. (Many colleges and universities require all FAFSA data be submitted to them by no later than March 1 of the year you will enroll or they will not guarantee the availability of aid for FAFSAs received after that date.) After processing the form, the financial aid office will then send your family an award letter that outlines the types and amount of aid that they will give to you during your first year of enrollment at that particular college or university. You should receive one award letter from each school that you were accepted to and to which you submitted a FAFSA. **Award letters are only good for one year; you must re-submit a FAFSA for each year you are enrolled as an undergraduate, graduate, and/or professional student at a college or university if you wish to continue receiving aid.**

Award letters can vary widely between schools, so families would be wise to design their own comparison chart by which to compare the amount of aid being offered by each school. A spreadsheet assembled in Excel or another similar program will do the trick – the most important thing is to list the dollar amounts for each award letter component (scholarships, grants, loans, etc.) side by side and then make a tally at the bottom. Read each award letter very carefully, as some schools have special terminology that makes unclear what is a grant and what is a loan; still other schools will build loans into their aid packages automatically whether you have expressed an interest in taking them or not.

For first-time FAFSA filers, the process can be daunting due to the amount of information required and the sometimes confusing nature of the questions asked. (Each time you re-file the FAFSA in ensuing years, many of the fields on the web form will pre-populate, saving you time and hassle.) In addition, much misinformation surrounds the filing process, as well as the process through which aid is awarded.

Perhaps you've heard the following:

- **Once the FAFSA is filed, you cannot make corrections.** The FAFSA can be filed using projected tax information if you have not yet completed your taxes for the current year. You must make sure to re-visit the site after filing to make necessary changes by logging into your FAFSA form and re-submitting it with the updated information. (You may also add additional schools that have accepted you in this way.) Keep in mind that any substantial changes in data will result in an adjusted award package – and the adjustment will not always go in your favor.

- **Saving money for college actually hurts a student's chances for receiving financial aid.** Saving money for college does *not* hurt a student's chances for receiving aid as long as the money is not in the student's name. Student assets are penalized more strongly in the awarding process than parents' – so 529 savings plans aren't harshly penalized, nor are parents' retirement accounts. (Grandparents who want to give monetary graduation gifts should do so *after* the student graduates high school. Trust funds should also be avoided if they are in the student's name.)

- **As long as your family isn't rich, you'll receive financial aid.** The FAFSA is designed to look more strongly at income as opposed to assets when it assesses a family's ability to pay for college, so if your parents' combined annual income is high but they don't have a lot of savings, your EFC could still be quite high – even if they are carrying a debt load related to car loans or other similar expenses. (FAFSA experts recommend pre-paying mortgages and paying down loan debt prior to filing when possible; it's also recommended to make any necessary large purchases – a new car, a new computer – before filing.)

- **If you demonstrate financial need on your FAFSA, the school has to meet it.** Interestingly, only a small number of public and private colleges and universities are committed to meeting one hundred percent of students' need; the rest meet as much of the need as they are able (or willing) to and leave a gap between the aid offered and the actual EFC. Students who wish to attend the institution will need to find a way to make up the gap on their own.

- **Savvy students can work their way through school.** Parents who worked their way through school prior to and during the 1980s didn't have to face the levels to which current tuition prices have risen and part-time jobs don't pay enough to cover them. Recent studies show that, while a few students can successfully navigate working and going to school, there's a stronger correlation between the amount of hours worked and college drop-out rates.

With the FAFSA, if the college or university has any lingering questions about your financial situation or feels that some part of the information you have provided is inaccurate or incomplete, your family may be selected to go through a process known as verification. Quite simply, verification requires that you submit copies of W2 statements, 1099 forms, and other tax paperwork so that they can "verify" the information contained in the FAFSA and give you the most accurate financial aid package possible.

Verification will most likely not be required, however, if your college or university uses their own internal financial aid supplement or asks applicants to submit an additional financial aid form like the CSS Profile. Administered by the College Board (who also administer the SAT), the Profile asks both tax-related questions that are similar in nature to the FAFSA, but also includes questions that are specific to the college or university's financial aid office – and are often more invasive. In addition, there is a charge to submit the CSS Profile that is usually between five and eighteen dollars; it isn't free like the FAFSA. Finally, some schools require that the CSS Profile be received in the fall around the same time that the student's application is submitted, as opposed to waiting until after January 1 like the FAFSA. (Institutions can set their own Profile deadlines internally, so you could potentially apply to five different schools that require the Profile and have five different due dates for the form.)

The other key difference between the CSS Profile and FAFSA is that, of the two, the Profile relies more heavily on the professional judgment of the school's financial aid staff than the FAFSA. That means that the school has the ability to look more closely at your individual financial circumstances in terms of the financial information that's been provided and can choose to award (or not award) funds based on what they believe will most benefit you as a student and their institution as a whole. Professional judgment can in fact be quite helpful in situations that are unusual and even schools that only require the FAFSA have an appeal process for families to use if they don't believe that their financial situation is accurately represented by the information contained in the FAFSA. In particular, sudden and unexpected circumstances can fall under this umbrella – the sudden loss of a parent, a parent's lost job, substantial medical expenses, bankruptcy, etc. If you fall within one of those categories, contact the financial aid office directly to determine what approach that particular school takes regarding special circumstances.

The final method through which you may consider paying a portion of your college costs is a **student loan.** There are three basic types of student loan – federal loans through the government, private loans through a bank or other lender, and loans through the college or university itself. (Note that loans through the college or university are the most rare.) As you consider whether or not loans will be part of your college funding plan, bear in mind that by 2012, the average student debt load in the United States had climbed to $29,400 – up from $26,600 in 2011. That's a ten and a half percent increase in just one year! So while there is nothing wrong with taking out some loans to assist with tuition, you must be extremely cognizant of exactly how much debt load you take on – in particular if you will pursue a graduate or professional degree beyond college or if your intended career is one that doesn't fall into a moderate or high income bracket. (If you intend to become a horse trainer, be aware that your first loan payments will be due at the same time you're trying to accumulate a clientele and build your business – an undertaking that is usually rather costly.)

The most common type of loan offered by the federal

government is a **Stafford Loan.** There are two forms of **Stafford Loan** – a **subsidized** version and an **unsubsidized** version. These loans are need-based and can only be awarded to those students who file a FAFSA, but they are not credit-based as some other student loans are. Both types of **Stafford Loan** have a 2014 fixed interest rate of 3.86 percent, but have divergent repayment terms. A **subsidized Stafford Loan** allows you to borrow up to $8,500 per year for your undergraduate enrollment and the government pays your interest as long as you are enrolled in school at least half-time. (This period of government-funded interest can carry over during any graduate or professional program that you might enter after you complete your undergraduate studies as long as you are enrolled at least half-time.) An **unsubsidized Stafford Loan** allows you to borrow up to $12,500 per year and does not require any repayments while you're enrolled in school (including graduate and professional programs) but *does* accrue interest over time, which needs to be repaid.

Most financial aid award letters feature a combination of both **subsidized** and **unsubsidized Stafford Loans.** It is your decision (in conference with your family) as to whether you will take one, both, or neither loan. When it comes time to graduate and begin to repay your loans, financial aid officers all recommend that you undergo an exit counseling session during which you can map out a plan for repaying all of your existing loans. (There are also a handful of loan forgiveness programs available, including a federal program for teachers and another for veterinarians.)

Though **Stafford Loans** are the most common student loans on the market and feature the lowest interest rate, many families also look into **Parents PLUS loans** as well. Also known as **Direct PLUS loans**, these are also federal loans that come from the U.S. Department of Education and feature a fixed interest rate. The primary difference between a **PLUS loan** and a Stafford Loan is that a **PLUS loan** requires a credit check and its receipt is credit-dependent. In addition, the parent or legal guardian filing the loan paperwork must be the adoptive or biological parent or step-parent of the student at the time of application. The loan is in the parent's name and he or she must sign a Master Promissory Note (MPN) to secure it and a loan origination fee will be charged. The funds must be directed toward direct and indirect educational expenses for the student; however, for student equestrians majoring in an equine-related field, this can be particularly helpful, as riding lessons and equipment can fall into the category of indirect expenses and be covered by a portion of the money.

With the economic downturn, private lenders largely stepped away from the student loan market, though many still exist and can be utilized if federal loans don't work out for one reason or another. Use extreme caution with private student loans, however, as the interest rates tend to be extremely high and there is very little loan forgiveness flexibility. (Parents should also know that, while you may wish for your son or daughter to take out the loan in his or her name, you will most likely need to co-sign the paperwork or the loan will not be granted.)

As college tuition prices continue to rise each year, the decision as to how you and your family will fund your education is one of the biggest you will make in your young life. Before you make your final decision and choose the school you will attend, be sure that you thoroughly understand each and every facet of your schools' award letters – even if it means scheduling a phone or in-person meeting with a financial aid officer from all of the schools that you were accepted to. While the educational programs at the school you eventually attend will shape your life's path from the moment you first set foot on campus as a freshman, so will the financial aspects of the decision you make.

10
THE HORSE – OF COURSE!
SHOULD I TAKE MINE TO COLLEGE WITH ME?

"What I really wish I had known [before college] was the number of opportunities there would be to be involved in the [equestrian] program without having your horse on campus."
Brittany, IDA dressage alumna

"I wish I would have been able to bring my horse with me in my first semester. Maybe it's because [my school was] unique for having the [Equestrian] Center, but the horse community is such an instant friend network that I think I would have adjusted to college life a lot faster if I had had [my horse] to help me prioritize my time and make a strong friend group right away."
Kate, IHSA western alumna

Often, the biggest decision that every high school equestrian faces as senior the transition to college approaches isn't related to the school that he or she will attend (though that decision is certainly a substantial one), but rather whether or not to take a treasured equine partner along for the ride. Each year, countless articles are published in popular equestrian magazines and featured online in social media and blogging communities on the subject, where you'll see that some students swear they wouldn't have survived their college careers without their horses nearby for support. Meanwhile, others confess that they had a lot more fun without constantly worrying about turnout and feeding options and the guilt that accompanies the inevitable day (or days) of the week when they couldn't make it to the barn. Some speak of selling horses midway through college because the stress and cost became too much and others refer to horses that were purchased *during* college to help them make the transition into adult life after graduation.

In short, there is no consensus on the issue.

Your decision whether take your horse with you on your college journey or leave him home should therefore be dependent on your individual circumstances. Before you can make a decision regarding your horse's future and how it will relate to your college career, however, there are several factors you must take into account:

- **What will you study?** It's a simple fact of college life that some majors are more time-consuming than others and will considerably reduce your time that is available for traveling to the barn and for riding. Some majors will also require you to spend time off-campus in co-op or internship experiences – potentially even sending you to an international location for a summer, a semester, or a year. Finally, many of your classes (regardless of your major) will require extensive work outside of lecture hours (labs, rehearsals, tutorials, small group projects, etc.). Regardless of your area of study, the general rule is that for every one hour of time in the classroom, you should spend two hours outside of class studying the material. If you have four classes per semester and each class meets three times per week, that's twenty-four study hours per week – an entire day!

- **Where is your school located?** Not every college campus is located in or near a horse-friendly environment, so you'll need to examine the surrounding area to see if there actually is a place that's suitable for your partner. Rural and suburban campuses can make this search relatively easy, but if your chosen campus is in a big city, how far outside of that city must you go to find boarding stables? How long will it take you to get to the barn on an average weekday? And if boarding is at a premium, how much will you be required to pay per month?

- **What will it cost to keep your horse on or near campus?**
  If you're already paying board for your horse, you might
  attend school someplace where board prices are cheaper –
  or you might wind up in an area where they are more
  expensive. In addition, consider the other expenses
  associated with keeping a horse at college – including your
  transportation costs to and from the barn. Because you're
  paying tuition in order to attend college, you also need to
  consider that your time has a monetary value while you're
  in school and you don't want to over-extend yourself
  outside the classroom to the extent that your grades begin
  to suffer.
- **What does your horse require and are those amenities
  available near your school?** The last thing you want to do
  is remove your horse from his happy home and find out
  that he's miserable because his needs aren't being met. For
  example, if yours is one who needs twenty-four hour
  turnout to be happy and the only stable near campus has no
  turnout, what will be the result when your horse makes the
  transition? Will the change in climate affect him if you
  move him from California to the East Coast? What feed
  and shoeing requirements does he have? Horses are
  certainly adaptable creatures and can thrive in many
  environments, but you'll be making some adaptations of
  your own and you might not be as attentive during that first
  semester to difficulties that he's facing.
- **What do you want your overall college experience to
  look like?** If you're very involved in clubs and other school
  activities during high school and want to continue at that
  level of involvement in college, you need to be aware that
  college organizations tend to be far more time-consuming
  than their high school counterparts. Student government,
  fraternities and sororities, and other types of clubs all
  normally meet after class hours – often during the evening
  or well into the night to accommodate members' busy
  schedules. They may also have extensive weekend
  activities that you will be asked to participate in and all of it
  can cut into your riding time. Still, the clubs and activities

you engage in are often the ones that you'll use on your resume when you apply for your first job after graduation, so it's important to consider all possibilities before you make the decision to limit your college experience to just your studies and time spent at the barn.

You might not know the answers to any of the above questions as you begin your college search, but if taking your horse to college is something that you want to consider as part of your final college decision, you'll need to take time periodically during your junior and (particularly) your senior year to talk with your parents and your trainer about your horse's needs and your equestrian goals in comparison to the schools that are at the top of your prospect list.

Remember, if becoming a part of your college's equestrian team is a top priority for you as part of your college choice, it isn't required that you take your horse to college with you at all. In fact, many coaches will discourage you from bringing your horse altogether so that your riding time will be freed up to catch ride the types of horses that you will encounter during competition. They don't want you won't have the distraction of worrying about your own horse's care to keep you from focusing on team goals and the improvement of your own riding skills.

(**Author's Note:** You may recall from Chapter Two that there are a handful of intercollegiate equestrian organizations that *do* require or encourage students to utilize their own horses, including the ANRC, NIRA, and the IEL. That's why it's very important to know what types of organizations will be available to you at your chosen institution before you consider how your horse may or may not fit into your college experience.)

If you and your family conclude that it *will* be feasible for your horse to accompany you when you make the move to college, you'll most likely be moving him or her to a boarding stable on or near campus. If your horse is currently boarded near your home, then you should be familiar with the practices of a standard boarding barn and you and your horse will simply need to adjust to the rhythms and culture of the new barn when you arrive. Your trainer or current barn owner/stable manager can work with the trainer or stable manager at the new barn to adjust your horse's feeding and turnout arrangements to that of the new place and get him or her on schedule with a new vet and farrier. If you're going to be taking lessons from a new trainer while you're away at school, your current trainer can help to prepare you for that transition as well and may even know the new trainer well enough that the two of them can update one another on your progress during the school year.

If you will attend a college or university with its own on-campus equestrian facilities and will board your horse there, you might encounter a very different environment from that which you're currently used to. Namely, many colleges have equestrian facilities that serve as the home to their equine major or an equine/animal science program as well as hosting the equestrian teams - and that type of environment can often result in a different type of horse keeping than you and your equine partner are used to. There may be certain accommodations that the two of you must make in your routine or adjustments to your horse's daily care that will be required as a result of living in this particular situation.

If you will board your horse at a college- or university-owned facility, it's important for both the well-being of your horse and your own expectations as a rider that you ask the following questions and understand why the answers will be important to you and your horse:

- **What types of riding are done at this facility?** Some schools limit their equestrian program or riding lesson offerings to only one or two disciplines even though they may open up their available stalls for boarding to riders from any discipline. This may not seem like an issue to you at first, but if you have always ridden in one discipline and find that the majority of the other riders participate in something completely different and foreign to you, you may encounter unanticipated tension during your daily training routine. Various stereotypes across the different equestrian disciplines tend to be easily brushed aside when you're only with riders who ride and compete in the same manner that you do, but if you're suddenly surrounded by people from other parts of the sport, the situation might bring those issues to the forefront. Many riders don't mind working around riders of other disciplines and can train well wherever they go, but others want to be surrounded by riders who think and train as they do and will be very uncomfortable in a situation where that isn't the case. Before you move your horse to campus, you'll need to decide what camp you belong to and plan accordingly.

- **How many boarding spots are open each year and what are the requirements to get one?** Some schools have a very limited amount of stalls available to student boarders and, as a result, open stalls up only to a certain population, such as members of the senior class or equine majors. If you're going to be a freshman and it's very important to you to keep your horse nearby, you might need to seek an alternative boarding arrangement with a local farm until a stall opens up on campus – perhaps for as long as your first three years. Some college programs might also have an application process for horses – they'll only accept geldings within a certain age group or will take only the horses with the best show records so that they can take you and your horse to regular (rated) shows under the umbrella of the college.

- **What is the responsibility of the horse owner to care for his or her horse?** Some college equestrian facilities are run just like the boarding stable that you and your horse might be coming from; that is, a barn crew comes in each morning to feed, turn out (where available), muck stalls, and do blanket changes where and when they are appropriate. Students need only worry about showing up to groom, tack up, and ride each day – or in some cases, they just show up to ride and even the grooming is included. Other facilities, however, require that the students put in a portion of the labor – they may have certain days per week that they are required to muck their own horses' stalls (sometimes for a reduction in board costs) or they may be the ones who are solely responsible for whether or not their horses receive turnout that day. Some college facilities are even wholly student-run in the form of a co-op, where the student stable manager helps set work hours for all of the students who keep a horse at the barn and people make time in their schedules to do their allotted chores each day.

- **Are boarded horses used as a part of the college major or riding program?** If your horse is going to live at the college's equestrian facility or equine center, part of the trade-off for his or her stall space might be a few hours of use per week in the school's lesson program or becoming a part of a study on feed and nutrition that the equine majors are conducting during a particular semester. Sometimes you can opt your horse out of these daily activities, but you might not get a choice as to whether he or she is required to be a part of the draw when your college hosts a home equestrian meet for the IHSA or IDA. If you're very particular about your horse and who is allowed to ride him or her, a college-owned facility that incorporates student horses into the program might not be an ideal situation.

- **What is the fee structure at this facility? How are charges assessed?** Some college equestrian programs bill on the same schedule as the institution itself; that is, all of your board and lesson fees for the semester will be due in a lump sum at the same time that your own tuition, room, board, and fees are due. You'll pay once in August and then again in January. Incidentals such as vet bills and farrier charges will be billed at the time of service. Other college programs bill monthly for all of your horse's charges in the previous month – board, vet, farrier, trailering fees, and any lessons you've taken or horse shows you've competed in. As you budget the costs of keeping your horse at school with you, it's important to know how and when the school will require you to pay.

  (**Author's Note:** It's also important to realize that, because the school owns and operates the facility, they reserve the right to withhold your diploma or final transcript after graduation if you owe money to the equestrian program or any other campus organization. This can hurt your chances for graduate school acceptance or your first job out of college if you over-extend yourself financially.)

- **What security measures are taken at the facility to protect horses, students, and equipment?** Most traditional boarding barns are quite secure, but college facilities often see more foot traffic from members of the public – as well as hosting more visitors overall – than other barns. It's important for you to know who has access to the facility at various times of the day and night, how often campus security or the local police patrol the area, and how the facility is monitored. Are there security cameras? Emergency phones? Is the facility secured behind a gate that only gives access to staff and boarders after a certain hour? How are pieces of equipment such as tack and horse trailers secured? And if a theft does occur, will you be covered under the college's insurance policy or should you carry your own?

- **During what hours will I have access to my horse?** College equestrian facilities sometimes have more limited hours than you may be accustomed to at your present boarding barn. In fact, some coaches or equestrian center directors might require that all riders be out of the barn at a certain hour to encourage everyone to focus diligently on their studies while others might allow students to be at the facility itself during all hours because their students prefer to study in the club lounge as opposed to the library. Riding hours might also be strictly monitored for safety reasons so that an instructor or other staff member will be present in the event of an accident. You might also have to contend with limited facility usage or access to your horse on weekends if the college hosts a full calendar of intercollegiate meets and local or regional open shows in their indoor and/or outdoor arenas.

- **How do horse owners get to the barn - by car? Bicycle? Is there a campus shuttle?** Even if your college or university owns the equestrian facilities, there is a good chance that they may be a bit of a distance from the main campus or located at one extreme edge that's far from the academic buildings and residence halls. It might not be feasible for you to walk there every day, so many campuses have a schedule of regular shuttles to and from the barn at no cost to you to make sure you can get there. Other riding programs encourage horse owners to bring their own car to campus and for horse owners and riders to carpool when possible. (If you plan to take your car with you, you should inquire about parking fees, parking lot assignments, and whether or not equestrians get priority in a campus-wide parking lottery.) And if you plan to get to the barn by bicycle each day and your college is located in a region that faces poor weather during the winter months, you'll need a plan for what you will do when the snow begins to fly.

Every college and university that owns its own equestrian center has rules, regulations, and practices that differ from their counterparts, so it's important that you keep careful track of which schools on your list have these facilities available and how each one operates. Make sure that you visit each facility when you visit the campus and that you have contact information for someone at the barn (ideally the director or stable manager) in addition to your admissions office contact. That way, you can stay in informed regarding the application process for a stall and ask questions about the boarding situation as you think of them.

As has been mentioned earlier in this chapter, if you plan to take your horse to school with you, whether he or she lives at the campus equestrian center or at a nearby barn, you'll need to incorporate transportation costs for both you and your equine partner into your overall college budget. It's a simple thing to do, but often students and families forget to take this into account when they outline what the additional charges will be when taking the horse along. Board, vet, farrier, and lessons are easy to put at the top of the list, but remember that you'll also need to account for a college parking fee at most institutions, as well as gas and regular maintenance for your vehicle (including tire rotations and oil changes). Emergency funds should also be allotted in case there is a bigger problem with the car and it needs substantial repair. In addition, remember to take an extra set of car keys with you to school in the event that you lock your keys inside – an incident that typically happens to most college equestrians when they're at the barn late on the night before a big horse show! Give the extra keys to a trusted roommate, your resident assistant, or the campus security office so that you won't need to call home or a towing company to come help you jimmy the lock.

If your parents are sending you to school with the truck and horse trailer so that you can be responsible for transporting your equine partner to competitions during the school year, you'll need to keep trailer maintenance and security in mind. You're your trailer is parked at the campus equestrian center or boarding stable, put a lock on the trailer hitch and make sure to keep all dressing rooms and tack compartments locked as well. (Horse trailers also make great storage units for things that won't fit in the tack room or things you're not using in your dorm room – but that plan only works if everything is locked securely to keep your possessions safe!)

It's also a good idea if you and your parents sign up for a membership to a trailering assistance company such as U.S. Rider who can offer you nationwide roadside assistance if you have any problems while in transit. Regular automotive assistance companies such as AAA will normally only help equestrians if their trailers are empty, but the equestrian-specific companies are trained to help when your horses are onboard. They are also able to help with truck repairs if you need help with just your vehicle. A membership can sometimes be costly, but it can pay off in spades when you and your horse make it safely to your destination!

Finally, if you will take your horse to school with you during the year but plan to return home during summer or semester breaks, you'll need to confirm with your boarding stable manager that this will be okay. At most facilities, they understand that college students will be away during certain times of the year but will return over the Christmas holidays (depending on the length of the break) and during the summer. Other barns, however, have a waiting list of potential boarders who will occupy stalls year-round and will not be willing to save your place while you're away. Working with your stable manager well in advance of your departure for college can help avoid unnecessary headaches during time periods that are supposed to be a vacation.

If you don't plan to take your horse to school with you, you will no doubt find many opportunities to ride either as part of your school's equestrian team or at a local facility with a lesson program. While your horse remains at home, however, you should have a plan in place to make sure that he or she is properly looked after. For students lucky enough to have their horses in the backyard, that could mean that a younger sibling or a parent takes over the barn duties – a transition that might require some instruction from you if they aren't already well-versed in the ways of horse husbandry. For students who board their horses at a nearby farm, work closely with the stable manager or your trainer to determine who will be allowed to ride your horse while you're at school and what goals you will set each year for the summers when you're home and riding again. Depending on what those goals are, your horse might need to go into full or partial training to keep fit; in other situations, if you plan to put your competitive career on a temporary hold during school, you might find it more advantageous to lease your horse out to another rider at the barn so that he or she is kept in regular work and you can defray some of the costs of owning your horse while you're paying college tuition.

Many students will also plan to finish out their high school careers and then sell their horse before leaving for college. The timing of this particular situation can often present other complications, as it's never certain when you advertise a horse for sale that it will sell by a certain date – or if it will sell at all! Your trainer can advise you on the best time to put your horse on the market, but you might need to prepare yourself for the moment that your horse sells *earlier* than planned and your summer show schedule gets cut short. Conversely, you might also find yourself packing for school without having sold your horse yet – and if that's the case, it's crucial that you, your parents, and your trainer have a plan ready to keep the horse in work and ready for prospective buyers while you're away. The horse sale market is never black and white when it comes to these matters, which is why it's absolutely essential that you plan for every eventuality.

11
MAKING THE TRANSITION

"Be open to learning new things in new ways from new instructors. Everyone can learn something from different instructors if you're not too closed-minded."
Ann, IHSA hunt seat and IDA dressage equestrian

After you complete all of the campus visits, fill out the forms, pore over the web sites, brochures, financial aid awards, and review final equestrian team statistics, inevitably the moment arrives for you to make your choice and select the one school you will attend. For some students, the moment arrives very early and they know even before all of the acceptance and financial information arrives that they have identified "the one." Their minds never waver from that dream school and everything falls neatly into place so that they can attend.

For others, the decision comes down to two top choices that both offer tremendous opportunities for growth and higher learning. When that occurs, the wavering and indecisiveness on the part of the affected student can drag into late spring and cause a high degree of stress along the way. Still, the deadline looms and a choice must be made. In fact, any student who was not accepted through a binding Early Decision policy or has not signed a National Letter of Intent as part of an athletic scholarship agreement is required to send an enrollment deposit to their chosen school by May 1 of their senior year. After that date, space availability in a school's first-year class and financial aid awards are no longer guaranteed.

(As though the indecisive students weren't under enough stress already!)

The May 1 date is formally known as the National Candidates' Reply Deadline and is the date observed by all National Association for College Admission Counseling (NACAC) member colleges and universities in the United States. It's a generally accepted rule that all decisions made by students on that date are final and there are a few formal processes in place to dissuade them from changing their minds over the summer. For example, schools will no longer return enrollment deposit money after May 1 to students who have a last-minute change of heart and enroll elsewhere – and for some colleges and universities, the deposit is a substantial sum of money, so it's important that students and families not take the final decision lightly.

Freshman housing is another big and often complex issue that incoming families have to grapple with as the May 1 deadline looms – in particular because many large, public universities have limited on-campus housing for all students and may have conflicting regulations in regard to dormitory selection. In these instances, if freshman are required to live on campus but housing space is at a premium, families will be strongly encouraged by the residential life office to place their housing deposit *prior* to May 1 in order to guarantee a room and bed in the residence hall that fall. These deposits may or may not be refundable for students who change their mind at the May 1 deadline - but because they don't fall under the umbrella of an enrollment deposit, they are not *technically* against the standards and practices of NACAC regarding the National Candidates' Reply Deadline. (It's a Catch-22 of modern higher education).

If you reach the spring of your senior year and find that you have one of these large schools with scarce housing still on (or at the top of) your prospective school list, it may well be in your best interest to pay the housing deposit as early as you can if you are able to. You'll just need to be prepared to forfeit the money later on if you make a different choice and enroll elsewhere.

For equestrians, once your final college decision is made and your enrollment and/or housing deposit has been sent to the appropriate campus offices, your next step is to contact all of the equestrian team coaches, advisors, or captains that you met or corresponded with during your college search to inform them of your final decision – especially for the schools that you will *not* attend.

Why is this so important?

First and foremost, it's polite. The equestrian world and the world of higher education are both realms in which reputations are of the utmost important – and *bad* reputations always seem to come back to haunt people at the most inopportune times. As such, taking just a few moments of your time to thank the people who helped steer you along your college search path and share with them where you will attend and what feature or program makes that school the right fit for you can go a long way toward building a good reputation with them - and might even help you out in the future. You never know when you might change your course of study and need to change schools in the middle of your college career. Or you might encounter one of those rival equestrian coaches after graduation when you're looking for a job in the horse industry. No matter how excited you are to have made your final decision, never burn a bridge along the way because you might be very surprised to discover later on that you need to cross it.

To communicate your final choice to the schools that you will not attend, a phone call, letter, or professionally-worded email will be sufficient to thank them for the time they spent with you, inform them where you will enroll in the fall (include the name of the school, don't just say "another college"), and wish them luck in the coming competition season. For the coach, advisor, or team captain located at the college that you *will* be coming to in the fall, a phone call, letter, or professionally-worded email will also inform them of your decision to attend.

(**Author's Note:** If you haven't signed a National Letter of Intent, a mere verbal commitment to a coach to let him or her know that you have chosen to join their program is *not* enough to finalize your enrollment status with the college or university itself. You must send the required monetary deposit and all necessary paperwork (some of which must be signed by you and a parent) to confirm enrollment with all of the necessary offices on campus.)

In particular, for varsity teams, the knowledge that you plan to join the team in the fall will be vital to the coaches as they plan their upcoming competition schedule. It will also be important for you to speak with a coach or team leader in regard to the tryout process that is required of you in order to secure a spot on the team, as well as learning what you'll need to do (or not do) over the summer in order to set yourself up to be successful as a first-year intercollegiate equestrian.

In particular, prospective IHSA riders should be fully aware *before* they sign up for a summer schedule of horse shows as to their exact standing within the IHSA rider placement scale. (The different levels for each discipline and some common coach strategies regarding student placements were outlined in Chapter Three. It's especially important to have this information if you are only one or two shows away from moving into a higher competition level within the IHSA structure. Speak with your future IHSA coach to see if he or she recommends that you remain at your current level or if they're fine with you moving up before you arrive on campus. By spring, as each IHSA coach generally has a good idea of which divisions will be filled by returning riders and where gaps will need to be filled. Having these conversations with your future coach early can also help you make a positive first impression and will reveal you to be an organized team player - which can be helpful for your own transition as you begin to think in terms of putting the team first. It's somewhat counterintuitive to the type of equestrian competition you might be familiar with and could take some getting used to.

If you have a specific goal with your home trainer and your own horse and it's something that you have worked toward for a long period of time, it's fine for that goal to supersede your interest in your placement on an intercollegiate team, however. College coaches certainly understand that every freshman team member arrives with their own history and that not all riders will drop everything they've done as a high school equestrian just because they've begun the transition to college. In fact, your new coach might be another supportive person to help you continue to achieve those outside goals. Nevertheless, it's valuable for you to know at what level you will be evaluated when you show up to school in the fall, as well as having an understanding of the skills that will be required of you as a college equestrian. No matter what decision you make regarding your last summer of showing before college, the most important thing for you to do is to make sure that you have had clear communication between you, your parents, and your trainers (both past and future) so that everyone is on the same page and can help you make the transition as smooth as possible.

Prospective NCEA athletes need to closely communicate their summer plans to their new coaches as well – though within the structure of the NCEA itself, much of the communication is automatically built into the process. In particular, if you will ride in the NCEA and are in a position to win prize money over the summer, you'll need to make sure that your expenses and winnings are properly tracked. Your future NCEA coaches may also start you on a summer workout regimen (which will continue through the school year under the supervision of university athletic trainers) and other preparatory activities. Each college equestrian program – regardless of governing body - is run a little bit differently so it's important that you communicate closely with your new coach once your decision to attend the school has been finalized so that you don't miss out on anything over the summer and can jump right in when the semester begins in the fall.

As a prospective intercollegiate equestrian, it's also important that you prepare yourself for your college career by accepting the possibility that the coach who recruited you and with whom you communicated during your college search might not be the same coach who greets you when you get to campus to begin school. As has been previously discussed, coaches changing programs happens with relative frequency in all college sports and even though you won't see equestrian coaching changes reported on ESPN's *Sports Center*, they occur just the same. The reasons that coaches change or leave programs aren't important – sometimes it's a new opportunity at a different school, sometimes it's a chance to run a private barn - but what you need to keep in perspective is the fact that when you choose your college as a high school senior, you're choosing the *whole* college – the academic program, the campus setting, the student body, the faculty, the staff, and the equestrian team. If only one thing changes between May 1 and the day you move into your residence hall room on campus in August and it's the team coach, then everything that's left will still be things that you liked about the school.

In fact, whether the coach who recruited you remains the same over the summer or changes, you'll still be riding in a new environment on new horses with new teammates *and* a new instructor when school begins. In some cases, riding in college may even be the first time that you've really ridden outside of the barn that you've ridden in since you first began as a young child. You might ride in your first group lessons or encounter warmblood horses for the first time. As such, nervousness is to be expected – as is the pressure that you will no doubt put on yourself to impress your new coach during those first few weeks of lessons. What's more, you won't be alone: every other freshman athlete and freshman student on campus will be going through a similar transitional experience as they begin to figure out where they will fit into their team and where they will fit in on campus. Remind yourself of that fact whenever you feel like you're the only one struggling because it's a guarantee that at least one other person - and probably more! – feel the same way. All it takes to overcome the initial nerves is time and experience and by the end of your first semester, you'll find that you feel far more secure about life as a college student.

You'll find that your first few weeks on campus will be made easier if you also adhere to the following guidelines:

- **Greet every new situation with an open mind.** Perhaps the new coach assigns you to ride the oldest-looking, ugliest horse in the barn. Rather than judge the horse by its appearance and go into your lesson with a negative attitude, make the assumption that the coach chose that horse for you for a particular reason and tell yourself that you're going to try to figure out what that reason is during the course of your lesson. Perhaps despite his appearance, the horse has the best flying changes in the barn and the coach wanted you to get a feel for them – or else he's sticky on the right lead and if you can get him to canter on it by the end of the lesson, the coach will put you on a more athletic horse for your next lesson. An open mind is going to get you a lot farther in the early days of your college riding career than a closed one.

- **Accept your new coach as the authority figure in your lessons and in the barn.** Every horse person runs their barn in their own unique way, so even though many barns have a lot in common, there are always subtle (and sometimes not so subtle) differences to be found. Likewise, every instructor has their own teaching style. It's safe to say, then, that you'll encounter many new rituals and ways of doing things when you begin to ride in college and it's crucial for you to understand that "different" isn't necessarily "wrong." As such, don't question what your new coach tells you in an effort to undermine his or her teaching process. So while it's certainly okay to ask questions that help further your understanding – for example, what the goal of a particular cavaletti exercise is or why the horse you're riding goes in a running martingale instead of a standing martingale – it's never okay to question the coach's authority. In the case of a coach who is a member of the staff of your college or university, he or she has been hired by the school for a reason – strength of teaching and mentorship, riding and coaching record, etc. – and has been granted permission by the institution to govern the program. In the case of a private barn owner who serves as team coach, he or she is generous enough to open up a private facility to assist you and your teammates in reaching your goals and does so purely by choice; it's important to be grateful for that opportunity. You don't necessarily have to *like* your coaches all of the time but you do need to respect them.
(**Author's Note:** The exception to this rule is any situation that is downright dangerous, reckless, or cruel to the people

or horses involved. If a situation involves bullying of riders, drugging of horses, or anything that you believe puts individuals in danger of being harmed in any way, you and your teammates must stand up for yourselves and your equine partners and report the coach's behavior to either the school, your NCEA/IHSA/IDA or organizational regional representative, or another authority figure immediately.)

- **Be respectful to your new teammates.** As stated in the last bullet point, you don't need to like all of the members of your new team, nor do you need to be friends with all of them in order to be successful. You all come from different backgrounds and have different personalities and if there are forty people on one team, there's a good chance that not every individual person is going to hit it off. Regardless of who you befriend on your new team, however, you must strive be a good teammate to everyone: always be on time to lessons and meets, follow team rules and regulations to the letter, pitch in when help is needed, and make sure that the team goals come before your own in both training and in competition. Successful teams are the ones who are able to reach this level of internal respect for one another – which is why it's also okay for you to expect the same level of respect and courtesy from your teammates that you show to them.

Remember also that, due to the unique nature of your sport, the horses at the barn where your team rides are your teammates too. Without them, you have nothing, so take the time and care to always groom them thoroughly before each lesson and make sure that each piece of tack is clean and appropriately fitted, that you warm up and cool down for the appropriate amount of time, and that you always leave the horse in either just as good or better condition than you found him or her when you arrived for your lesson. Long after you've forgotten how many ribbons you won or points you accumulated, you and your human teammates will remember the names and personalities of the school horses you rode, so make the memories of those horses the best that you possibly can.

- **Recognize that everyone has bad days – and the secret to your success will be in how you manage them.** Every college student – especially those in their freshman year – will have rough patches. You might be homesick (or horse sick) or you might make silly mistakes during your first few weeks at school. You might even misread the signals that your horse gives you at team tryouts and fall off in front of everyone. It's happened to students who have come before you and it will happen to students who follow; the main thing to keep in mind is that, in a few weeks, you *will* become accustomed to life in college and life as a college equestrian and things *will* get better. Falling off that horse in tryouts isn't a disaster unless you allow it to become one by giving it power over the decisions you make next. If you stand up after that fall and decide that you can't achieve your goal of making the team anymore, you'll find yourself in the middle of a self-fulfilling prophecy and you might miss the opportunity to ride on the team at all for the next four years. (Remember, coaches want riders with good attitudes more than anything.) So instead of beating yourself up, why not laugh at the mistake and move past it? Ask your coach to put you back on the horse for another try and repeat one of George Morris' famous mantras: "On or hospital. *On or hospital."*

- **Find a mentor as an underclassmen and take the time to become one as an upperclassmen.** Everyone needs guidance at transitional points in their lives and college is a significant one. If you can find someone who has been through the process or simply understands it better than you do and is willing to share that information to help smooth your way, it can help make that first semester at school far easier than it otherwise might be. Perhaps there's a team captain who makes you feel welcome and comfortable when you attend the first team or club meeting or else the coach or another member of staff is always very patient in answering your questions. While you don't necessarily want to attach yourself to that person and that person alone, it's okay to seek his or her counsel in situations where you're unsure or need some support. Later, when the tables have turned and *you're* the upperclassman, remember the awkwardness of those first few weeks and allow yourself to be open and welcoming to help the new members of the team find their way as well. A network of mentorship is part of what makes teams strong and can go a long way toward building a team's legacy and a bond across the class years. Teams with a particularly strong structure of this sort can even reach beyond graduation, with alumni looking to hire recent graduates who shared that same team experience they remember fondly – or even alumni who look to give back in the form of a financial donation or high quality school horse that will benefit the entire program.

A positive attitude isn't the only thing you need to pack when it comes time to leave home and head to campus either. Most college and university residential life offices will send or post a list of common items that you will need for your dorm room – as well as a list of things that you should leave at home. Each campus has slight variations on what is and is not allowed, so consult the lists carefully before you make any purchases or accept gifts from relatives. Riders too must make sure that the equipment and items that they bring along to campus with them are appropriate and you'll find that most coaches and equestrian team captains are forthright about what you will need for the year.

Common items that freshman college equestrians need to bring to campus with them include:

- **Appropriate schooling attire for your discipline**. (Generally this means breeches and boots or half-chaps for hunt seat, dressage, and eventing riders and jeans and boots for western riders).
- **A helmet that is ASTM-SEI certified**. Due to recent head injury cases and changing rules across all disciplines, a helmet should be packed and brought with you no matter what your discipline. Don't allow one

fall to derail your college career or the course of your entire life.

• **Hairnets if you need them**. Some barns will stock them for riders but others won't. Make sure that your hair is always neatly secured for your lessons whether your coach requires it or not. Doing so shows respect and care for the team and the organization.

• **Spurs and a crop (where applicable).** The NCEA, IHSA, and IDA all have specific rules governing the use of spurs and whips so if you have your own, bring them with you and your coach will let you know if they are legal for competition. (In addition, there may be particular horses at the barn that require use of one type of item or another.) If you do not have spurs or a crop, **do not purchase them before you arrive** at college; most teams share them or encourage you to purchase a particular brand/size and you'll want to be sure you get the right ones.

• **Your show clothes**. Even if your team tryout isn't held until you arrive on campus (usually true for IDA and IHSA teams), the first meet is often one or two weeks after the team is announced. In particular if you are far from home, don't take a chance on getting them shipped, just pack them. (And if you don't make the team fall semester, there's always the possibility you will do an open or rated show outside of the intercollegiate structure and will still need them.) If, however, you don't own show clothes, don't purchase them before you get to school, as some teams have required colors and/or clothing brands that all riders must have. You don't want to spend the money to get all of your clothing only to find out a month later that you need an entirely new wardrobe!

• **Garment bags and other items in which to transport your riding clothes**. In particular, a garment bag for show clothes, a helmet case or box, and a boot case or bag are the most useful items for college students – and the sturdier, the better! At college meets, there aren't usually a lot of places to keep your clothes up and out of the dirt, so make sure you have some equipment to make that task easier.

• **Appropriate barn footwear.** College equestrians are often the ones who run their home shows and they spend a great deal of time volunteering to assist with the school horses at their home barn both on regular weekdays and weekends as well. As such, always make sure you have paddock boots, cowboy or work boots, and/or Wellingtons available so that you can be safe at the barn at all times. (Sturdy winter boots with a warm lining will also be necessary if your school is located in a region of the country that sees cold, snowy weather in the winter months.)

• **A padlock.** Most barns will assign you to a tack or equipment locker or will have one available for rent but you will need to provide your own lock for security. Keep the combination or a spare key somewhere handy over the holiday and summer breaks so that you don't forget it and need to remove the lock with bolt cutters. (Consider keeping the spare with the stable manager or sharing the combination with him or her so that you can ask for help if you're in a bind.)

Items to leave at home or to consult with your coach or teammates about include:

• **Your own tack.** Some college programs will allow you to bring your own saddle to use in lessons (provided it fits the horse that you've been assigned to that day). Others prefer that you use the appropriate saddle for each school horse – especially as you'll be using a strange saddle at every meet when you draw a new horse. Be sure to check with your new coach regarding his or her policy on tack, as there may not be enough storage space for your saddle at the barn and you don't want to risk theft (or the wrath of your roommate) by keeping it in dorm room or vehicle.

• **Grooming equipment.** Unless you're bringing your own horse with you, the same rule applies to grooming equipment. Most school horses have all of their own necessities already so you can leave yours at home.

• **Any equipment too large to fit in a tack locker.** Many barns have limited storage areas for riders and/or boarders. If the tack lockers at your new barn are going to be too small for a piece of equipment that you own, it's always best to leave it home.

• **Other pets.** Though some colleges have incorporated pet-friendly residence halls into their offerings for students, it's not common and pets are frowned upon if they don't live in aquariums. If you live off campus and are allowed have a dog, however, it's best not to bring it to the barn with you right away until you know your coach's rules regarding pets.

Though leaving for college is often a nerve-wracking and uncertain time in your life, it's also one that is exciting and full of possibility and opportunity. The people you will meet on campus and as a result of your involvement with an equestrian team (or any of the college organizations that you join) will become your lifelong friends. You'll share many fun experiences and memories with them long after you've graduated and life has taken you in different directions so it's important not to let the fear of the unknown prevent you from trying new things and meeting new people in your first weeks on campus. You might surprise yourself by discovering a new interest, making a new best friend, or finding your academic passion if you're bold enough to explore – and that's what making the transition to being a full-fledged college student is all about.

SOME NOTES FOR PARENTS

"I would have liked more letters from my parents. Everyone loves letters and packages." **Kate, IHSA western alumna**

Parents, if you've read all the way through this book and have just now reached this chapter or even if you're just opening its pages for the first time and have turned specifically to this section, it's important that you realize one important fact:

Your role in the college search process of your son or daughter is more important than that played by all of the counselors, coaches, teachers, trainers, and mentors that your student knows *combined*. In fact, in a 2013 study of more than three thousand recent high school graduates, nearly sixty percent of the students indicated that their parents influenced where they would apply to college and seventy-seven percent stated that their parents were influential in determining where they would ultimately enroll. That's a great deal of power to possess and places you in the position of striking a delicate balance between being a supportive parent and actively playing one of those roles of counselor, coach, teacher, trainer, and mentor. It isn't to be taken lightly – but you shouldn't allow it to overwhelm you either. The example you set during the college search and decision process can do a lot to help reduce your child's stress and trepidation regarding the future.

Whether your child has been involved in equestrian sports for the whole of their young lifetime or has only recently discovered a love for it, you have no doubt come to fully comprehend the influence that their passion for horses and riding has over nearly every decision that they make in their daily lives. In fact, you may have discovered your own unwavering support for their riding careers because you've seen that time in the saddle brings them joy and because the skills they have acquired as a result of this

159

dedication have been so character-forming. They know about organization, time management and good leadership, and they have the confidence to take appropriate risks and challenge themselves in new situations. As a result, the money spent, the hours in the car at the crack of dawn on a cold Saturday morning in February, and the days spent in the rain by the side of the show ring have all been worth it. Your child has developed into a mature and wonderful young adult through equestrian sports and there's no reason that you can see to remove them from that path during their college years.

Yet it would be unfair to assume that you aren't nervous about the prospect of college. In fact, sending your student to college can feel a lot like giving them a leg up onto a horse and sending them out for a lesson, a clinic, or a show. You must trust in the skills they have learned, the knowledge they possess, and their own confidence when you send them out to have a safe and competitive jumping round or a cross-country run that's within the time allowed. Your heart might be in your throat and your breathing might be shallow the entire time they're out there, but when you see the look of triumph on their faces at the end, you realize that your fears were unfounded. They have trained for this moment and are prepared to face the challenge ahead.

Your nervousness isn't without justification, however. As a horse show mom or dad, you have come to understand that horses - like life - can be unpredictable at times. Sometimes the trustworthy and unflappable schoolmaster spooks for no apparent reason at the flower box at C and bolts across the arena. On occasion, the rock solid equitation horse gets a bad distance and crashes through an oxer, sending poles and wings flying and depositing the rider in the sand. But your son or daughter has spent countless hours practicing and preparing for these unexpected occurrences so that when disaster occurs they're able to deal with it effectively and move on. The dressage rider gets control of her horse, goes back to C, and repeats the movement she was headed for when the spook happened. The equitation rider stands up, dusts himself off, and vows to read the line better next time. You as a parent have a moment of fear and trepidation out of sheer reflex, but once you see that your child knows how to deal with the situation – and *is* dealing with it – all should return to normal.

If you take nothing more away from this book and this chapter, please take the knowledge that you are a unique parent in the world of college admissions because you are better-equipped in many ways to deal with sending your child off to college than your peers. You have watched your child win and lose from the rail of countless horse shows. You have straightened ties and braided hair and shined boots as wells as wiping tears, giving supportive hugs, and even taking occasional trips to the emergency room. You have watched your son or daughter master the art of convincing a twelve hundred pound nonverbal animal to do things that aren't necessarily within its nature – jumping fences, performing canter pirouettes, rolling back and sliding into stops. If they have the confidence in their ability to succeed as an equestrian, they are well on their way to becoming successful college students.

In fact, the most important things that you can do to support your son or daughter in the search for a college and later in the decision process aren't necessarily that different than those that you've already exercised as a successful horse show parent. You should adhere to the following guidelines:

- **Be honest about finances from the beginning.** For many families, the financial side of the equation is the single biggest factor influencing where a student enrolls in the fall. If you're open and up front with your child before a single potential school is placed on his or her list, it will make the entire process that much smoother for everyone. Conversely, telling your child that they shouldn't worry about the cost of a school – that it's your problem to deal with and they should go with their heart – is fine if it's the truth, but if it isn't, the whole thing can blow up in your face after financial aid award letters are released in the spring and their dream school isn't a financial possibility. There's no better way to teach your children to deal with money and be fiscally responsible than to be honest from the beginning and set your family up for college decision success from Day One. Remember, many young riders are already familiar with household budgeting and financial planning if they've talked through the year's horse show budget with you previously and the college talk can be a continuation of that ongoing conversation.

- **Allow your student to influence the search process as much as possible.** Inevitably, you most likely have a list of potential schools in mind for your son or daughter that may or may not match the one that they're envisioning. Your alma mater, a popular state public, or a prestigious Ivy League school might seem like everything you've ever wanted for your child and might even offer the right academic and/or equestrian opportunities as well – but unless he or she has demonstrated some form of interest in the school, it might not make the final cut when the list is completed. If you want your son or daughter to trust you as you walk through the process, you cannot force your opinions into the situation. It's going to be far easier on everyone if you are able to maintain the perspective that, as long as he or she is happy and excited about the school that is eventually chosen, there's no way your student will make a bad decision.

- **Don't monopolize campus tours or conversations with admissions or coaching personnel.** Higher education news and blogs are consistently filled with stories about so-called "helicopter parents" and the newest incarnation, the "snowplow parent" who insert themselves so forcefully into the admissions and recruitment process that the school really has no idea who the student is but they are *quite* familiar with the parents! If your child is going to take ownership of the search process (see the previous bullet point), it's important that they take ownership of every part of it – which means that when they have questions for college staff members, they must write their own emails, make their own phone calls, and respond to all school inquiries on their own. (Remember, these are the same students who jump 1.35 meter fences and can gallop at a pace of 550 meters per minute cross-country, so picking up the phone should really be no big deal.) If you have questions of your own, find the appropriate time and method with which to ask them and don't pre-empt your student's part in the process.

- **Don't take the process personally.** Admissions decisions occasionally defy all logic and reason when examined from the perspective of an outsider. Likewise, every college coach has his or her own preferences when it comes to putting together a team each year. On paper, your son or daughter might be a perfect fit for the university that later denies his or her application – just as on paper, he or she might be a great fit for the equestrian team that passes your student over in favor of a different rider. Every parent wants their son or daughter to be accepted to top schools and competitive riding teams, but dreams and reality don't always come together the way people want them to. Your child will have options available when it comes to both college attendance and equestrian team selection, so the best thing you can do is to embrace those institutions that embrace your student and forget about the ones that turn them down. If you maintain a positive outlook and avoid letting personal disappointment cloud the issue, chances are very good that your son or daughter will be able to do the same.

As you've probably already learned as a horse show parent (or simply as a parent in general), a healthy dose of perspective can go a long way to ensuring that your son or daughter learns to navigate success and disappointment in equal measure during their growing up years. The college search process tends to put that perspective to the test for nearly every family who goes through it each year, but if you've practiced enough by this point, you should be well-equipped to weather the storm. What's more, you'll also be equipped to help your son or daughter weather it alongside you.

FINAL COMMENTS

Whether you're an equestrian, a student athlete of any kind, or simply just a high school senior, the search for the right fit college can often seem like an insurmountable task. Indeed, equestrians sometimes face a more uphill battle than their peers in traditional sports if only because in many ways, they have a wider variety of options and opportunities available to them as they move from the ranks of junior equestrians to intercollegiate equestrians. But as with everything else, a little bit of time and information can go a long way toward your success. Know yourself, set some reasonable and achievable goals, and take the time to digest the information that's out there and is available to you. Do some dedicated research, ask people for help, and make no assumptions along the way that might throw you off track. If you stay true to your preferences and your goals, you will have plenty of wonderful college (and riding) offers on the table for your post-high school years and you'll graduate college with a handful of horse show ribbons as well as a top-notch education, lifelong friends, and priceless memories.

SPECIAL THANKS

This book would never have materialized on the page without the generous assistance, support, and knowledge of the following groups and individuals, to whom I owe the utmost gratitude. Listed (mostly) alphabetically, they are:

Natalie Burton, Interim Head Equestrian Coach of Southern Methodist University. Thank you for your advice and insight on Chapter Seven.

George Halkett, Equestrian Director of Stoneleigh-Burnham School. George is a longtime mentor and friend who would *never* dream of telling me how to do my job. He is the one I quoted as saying, "Riding is supposed to be hard; if it wasn't, they'd call it bowling" that was featured in the introduction. (He would also like you to know that he is an excellent horseman *and* bowler.)

David Hawsey, Vice President of Enrollment Management at Gardner-Webb University brought me into the world of higher education as a wide-eyed undergraduate intern and demonstrated all of the possibilities that working in college admissions presented. He later gave me the opportunity to put my education into practice and led our admission team with his excellent example every single day. My deepest thanks to you, sir.

Thanks to **Tom Jaworski** of Quest College Consulting, a supportive colleague, reader of my initial manuscript, writer of insightful emails, and (most importantly) a fellow Starbucks aficionado.

Sloane Milstein of College Riding 101 is a friend, a sounding board, a college professor, and writes a heck of a helpful book herself.

Lannis Smith was a terrific IHSA team captain and is now a fully graduated and successful grown up. (I'm so proud of you!) She has always been a talented photographer as well and my deepest thanks go to her for providing the cover image for this book.

The Entire **IECA Summer Training Institute Class of 2012** deserves my thanks for being the best coworkers a girl could have. I can't wait to see all of you at the next conference!

I cannot fail to mention the **staff of the Physical Plant at Spring Arbor University**, who have spent countless hours entertaining me (Has anyone seen #12?) and have provided a perspective on higher education in America that has been more helpful than any of you know.

Thank you also to my former students **Ann, Kate, Lauren, Brittany, and Ruthie,** who generously shared their thoughts on the college equestrian experience and allowed me to print their words so that others could learn from them.

Mom and Dad. This book is dedicated to you because it's probably more yours than it will ever be mine.

RESOURCES
Preface
Alice in Wonderland quote: https://www.goodreads.com/work/quotes/2933712-alice-in-wonderland-alice-s-adventures-in-wonderland-1

Is College the Right Choice for Me?
College enrollment in 2013: http://nces.ed.gov/fastfacts/display.asp?id=372

Percentage of students who are undecided:
http://www.nytimes.com/2012/11/04/education/edlife/choosing-one-college-major-out-of-hundreds.html?_r=0

Percentage of students who change their major:
http://borderzine.com/2013/03/college-students-tend-to-change-majors-when-they-find-the-one-they-really-love/

Earning potential:
http://www.nytimes.com/2014/05/27/upshot/is-college-worth-it-clearly-new-data-say.html?_r=0

Women's earnings:
http://usgovinfo.about.com/od/censusandstatistics/a/womenpayed.htm

Graduate debt load:
http://www.usatoday.com/story/money/personalfinance/2013/12/04/class-of-2012-student-debt-load/3867575/

Average time to degree: http://nces.ed.gov/fastfacts/display.asp?id=40

Gap year:
http://www.insidehighered.com/views/2014/01/16/more-students-should-take-gap-years-going-college-essay

I Won't Go to College if I Can't Ride
IHSA teams:
http://www.ihsainc.org/

NCEA:
http://varsityequestrian.com/

NCAA emerging sports:
http://www.ncaa.org/about/resources/inclusion/emerging-sports-women

NCEA warm up: http://www.collegiateequestrian.com/about/history.html

IDA history:
http://teamdressage.com/about-us/history-of-ida

IDA scoring:
http://teamdressage.com/docs/default-source/default-document-library/ida-rules-2013-2014.pdf?sfvrsn=2

ANRC teams:
http://anrc.org/what_is_anrc/participating-colleges-and-universities/

ANRC format:
http://anrc.org/wp-content/uploads/2013/12/2014-Prize-List-emailed.pdf

Polo teams:
http://uspolo.org/wp-content/uploads/2013/10/IC-by-State-9.24.13.pdf

Polo rules:
http://uspolo.org/wp-content/uploads/2012/09/tourn2013.pdf

Rodeo history:
http://www.collegerodeo.com/history.asp

Rodeo teams: http://www.collegerodeo.com/membership/Membership.asp

Rodeo format:
http://www.collegerodeo.com/downloads/2014/Rulebook%202013-2014.pdf

IEL history:
http://intercollegiateeventing.com/IEL/History.html

IEL scoring:
http://intercollegiateeventing.com/IEL/F.A.Q..html

ISSRA founding:
http://www.intercollegiatesaddleseat.com/

ISSRA format: http://www.intercollegiatesaddleseat.com/horseshows.html

AQHA judging:
http://www.aqha.com/AQHYA/Content-Pages/Activities/AQHA-World-Championship-Collegiate-Horse-Judging-Contest.aspx

Judging format:
http://www.aqha.com/Showing/World-Show/Blog/11162012-AQHA-CollegiateJudging-Contest.aspx

Judging format:
http://www.oqha.com/aaqhc/contests/more-youth-contests

AIEC format:
http://www.aiecworld.com/?page_id=165

USPC membership:
http://www.ponyclub.org/?page=membership

USPC mission:
http://www.ponyclub.org/?page=PCProgram#Join

Understanding Life as a College Equestrian
Definition of varsity:
http://www.merriam-webster.com/dictionary/varsity

Big Colleges, Small Colleges, Urban, Rural – How Do I Know What's Best for Me?
Definition of college:
http://www.merriam-webster.com/dictionary/college

Definition of university:
http://www.merriam-webster.com/dictionary/university?show=0&t=1391107649

Explanation of 501 c 3:
http://www.aau.edu/WorkArea/DownloadAsset.aspx?id=14246

For profit college:
http://www.ncsl.org/research/education/for-profit-colleges-and-universities.aspx

Public university: http://collegeapps.about.com/od/glossaryofkeyterms/g/public-university-definition.htm

Private college: http://collegeapps.about.com/od/glossaryofkeyterms/g/private-university-definition.htm

Ivy League:
http://etcweb.princeton.edu/CampusWWW/Companion/ivy_league.html

Harvard accept rate 2014: http://www.businessinsider.com/ivy-league-acceptance-2018-2014-3

Liberal arts college: http://collegeapps.about.com/od/glossaryofkeyterms/g/liberal-arts-college-definition.htm

Community college: http://collegeapps.about.com/od/glossaryofkeyterms/g/Community-college-definition.htm

U.S. Service Academies: http://collegeapps.about.com/od/choosingacollege/tp/military-academies.htm

U.S. Service Academy admissions: https://www.collegemapper.com/blog/2012/09/military-academies-how-to-get-in/

Eighty percent rule in college admissions: http://www.centerforpubliceducation.org/Main-Menu/Staffingstudents/Chasing-the-college-acceptance-letter-Is-it-harder-to-get-into-college-At-a-glance/Chasing-the-college-acceptance-letter-Is-it-harder-to-get-into-college.html

College selectivity: http://highereddatastories.blogspot.com/2013/09/whats-all-fuss-about.html

Preliminary financial aid information: http://studentaid.ed.gov/

Preliminary student loan information: https://studentloans.gov/myDirectLoan/index.action

Social media checkups: http://allfacebook.com/kaplan-college-admissions-officers-2013_b126570

Primary source definition: http://www.princeton.edu/~refdesk/primary2.html

The Campus Visit – When, Why, and How?

Official visit: http://www.collegiateequestrian.com/students/ncaarules.html

170

I Want to Be an Officially Recruited Athlete – How Do I Achieve My Goal?

NCAA eligibility:
http://fs.ncaa.org/Docs/eligibility_center/Quick_Reference_Sheet.pdf

Amateur athlete: http://www.collegiateequestrian.com/students/faq.html

Coaches:
http://www.collegiateequestrian.com/membership/prospectiveuniversities.html

Coach contacts: http://www.collegiateequestrian.com/students/faq.html

Average NCEA team size:
http://www.collegiateequestrian.com/membership/prospectiveuniversities.html

National Letter of Intent:
http://www.nationalletter.org/index.html

Will Being an Equestrian Help My Chances of Being Admitted?

SAT:
http://sat.collegeboard.org/about-tests/sat/why-take-the-test

SAT or ACT:
http://www.petersons.com/college-search/test-prep-act-sat.aspx

Khan Academy test preparation:
https://www.khanacademy.org/sat

Sending scores:
http://sat.collegeboard.org/scores/send-sat-scores

Sending scores:
http://www.actstudent.org/scores/send/

SAT score choice:
http://sat.collegeboard.org/register/sat-score-choice

Universal College Application: https://www.universalcollegeapp.com/

Common Application:
https://www.commonapp.org/Login#!PublicPages/History

Rolling admissions:
http://collegeapps.about.com/od/admissionstimeline/a/rolling.htm

Definition of scholarship: http://dictionary.reference.com/browse/scholarship

Tuition discounting: http://www.nytimes.com/2013/12/26/education/getting-out-of-discount-game-small-colleges-lower-the-price.html?pagewanted=1&_r=2&hp&

NACAC good practices:
http://www.nacacnet.org/about/Governance/Policies/Documents/SPGP_9_2013.pdf

I'm Accepted! What Scholarships are Available to Me and Will I Be Eligible for Financial Aid?

Financial need:
http://www.usnews.com/education/blogs/the-scholarship-coach/2012/07/19/12-college-financial-aid-terms-defined

FAFSA changes:
http://studentaid.ed.gov/fafsa/next-steps/correct-update#changes-to-federal-school-codes

FAFSA myths/strategies: http://www.reuters.com/article/2014/01/06/us-column-weston-collegemyths-idUSBREA050KV20140106

FAFSA myths/strategies: http://www.finaid.org/fafsa/maximize.phtml

FAFSA verification:
http://www.finaid.org/fafsa/verification.phtml

CSS Profile:
http://www.finaid.org/fafsa/cssprofile.phtml

Average student debt: http://money.cnn.com/2013/12/04/pf/college/student-loan-debt/

Stafford Loans:
http://www.staffordloan.com/stafford-loan-info/

Parents PLUS loans:
http://www.direct.ed.gov/parent.html

The Horse of Course – Should I Take Mine With Me?

Study hours: http://www.usu.edu/arc/idea_sheets/pdf/estimate_study_hours.pdf

U.S. Rider:
http://www.usrider.org/index2.html

Some Notes for Parents

Rogers, G. (2014). "How Students Really Decide." *The Journal of College Admission* p. 49-50.

ABOUT THE AUTHOR

Randi C. Heathman is an independent educational consultant whose decade of experience in college admissions and enrollment and lifetime involvement in equestrian sports give her a unique and beneficial platform from which to advise students and families.

Heathman holds a B.A. in English and an M.A. in communication studies/leadership. She honed her craft as senior assistant director of admission at Albion College (Albion, Michigan) while also working extensively with their equestrian program from its opening in 2004. In fact, Heathman's undergraduate Honors thesis was the impetus for the creation of the equestrian program at Albion and it was her work with that program that helped her gain an understanding of intercollegiate equestrian sports of all kinds. Her years of experience in college admissions also gave her tremendous insight into what details go into shaping a school's freshman class.

At present, Heathman is the only practicing educational consultant who includes both enrollment and intercollegiate equestrian experience on her resume. She is an associate member of the Independent Educational Consultants Association (IECA), a member of the Higher Education Consultants Association (HECA), the National Association for College Admission Counseling (NACAC), and travels to many college campuses each year in addition to attending as many professional development conferences as time allows. She is also a popular speaker at events including the College Preparatory Invitational Horse Show and Dressage 4 Kids Midwest.

Growing up in the Midwest herself, Heathman tried a number of disciplines before settling on dressage. She is a member of the United States Equestrian Federation (USEF) and United States Dressage Federation (USDF). She is a USDF bronze and silver medalist.

To learn about her services or book a speaking engagement, visit her web site at www.equestriancollegeadvisor.com.

31234097R00106

Made in the USA
Middletown, DE
29 December 2018